wanted

PEARSON
Prentice Hall
BUSINESS

Books that make you better

Books that make you better. That make you *be* better, *do* better, *feel* better. Whether you want to upgrade your personal skills or change your job, whether you want to improve your managerial style, become a more powerful communicator, or be stimulated and inspired as you work.

Prentice Hall Business is leading the field with a new breed of skills, careers and development books. Books that are a cut above the mainstream – in topic, content and delivery – with an edge and verve that will make you better, with less effort.

Books that are as sharp and smart as you are.

Prentice Hall Business.
We work harder – so you don't have to.

For more details on products, and to contact us, visit
www.pearsoned.co.uk

wanted

How to become *the* most wanted employee around

David Freemantle

PEARSON

Prentice Hall

BUSINESS

Harlow, England • London • New York • Boston • San Francisco • Toronto • Sydney • Singapore • Hong Kong
Tokyo • Seoul • Taipei • New Delhi • Cape Town • Madrid • Mexico City • Amsterdam • Munich • Paris • Milan

PEARSON EDUCATION LIMITED

Edinburgh Gate

Harlow CM20 2JE

Tel: +44 (0)1279 623623

Fax: +44 (0)1279 431059

Website: www.pearsoned.co.uk

First published in Great Britain in 2009

ISBN: 978-0-273-72491-9

British Library Cataloguing-in-Publication Data
A catalogue record for this book is available from the British Library

Library of Congress Cataloging-in-Publication Data
A catalog record for this book is available from the Library of Congress

To Marilou 'Mhay' Flores Regalario

CONTENTS

Preface

At the end of 2007 I emigrated from the UK to the Philippines and made an attempt to retire. I was 65. As the year wore on I found myself increasingly busy presenting business seminars across Asia. So on 2 August during a three-hour flight from Singapore I did what all good retired people are supposed to do, I sat back and reflected on my life. I realised I still had an urge to write. I had already written books that focused on success, whether as a manager or in delivering customer service, but what next? On 2 August 2008 I did not have an answer.

On 3 August 2008 it came. Out of nowhere a new idea popped into my mind as I lie in bed unable to sleep. Having focused on managers and customers it occurred to me I should write a book on how employees could become successful. It would apply to people who have a job as well as those looking for one. It was self-evident that some people are much more adept than others at staying in a job or getting a new one. So I decided on this subject for my book. I would draw upon a lifetime of experience to help.

The following morning I started putting pen to paper (or fingers to keyboard) and over the coming weeks drafted a few chapters together with an outline of the book which, after much agonising, I entitled *Wanted*.

I emailed the idea to Rachel Stock and Samantha Jackson at Pearson Education (who had published some of my earlier works) and happily they agreed to it.

This was the first week of September 2008. This coincided with the bailout of Fannie Mae and Freddie Mac in the USA and then the bankruptcy of Lehman Brothers and the sale of Merrill

Lynch. A week or two later the stock markets were crashing and the whole world was precipitated into a global financial crash. It all happened very quickly. Despite brave talk from politicians the crisis evolved over the following months into a recession that is (still) afflicting many countries. In November 2008 533,000 jobs were lost in the US labour market alone.

By December 2008 it seemed that the situation was dire. Many governments were trying to 'bail out' their economies with 'stimulus packages' and fear spread amongst the world's population that the employed would become unemployed, and that the unemployed would not be employed again for long while. In March 2009 the US unemployment rate rose to a 25-year high of 8.5 per cent with 663,000 jobs axed during the month.

It seemed to me that my book was increasingly relevant in such circumstances. Even during the worst recessions there are still job vacancies although fewer in number. So it would be wrong to assert that 'It is impossible to get a job in a recession'. The people who I describe as *Wanted* in this book are those who succeed in staying in jobs, or in getting new jobs – even during a recession. These are people who have developed a wide range of skills, knowledge, experience and attributes that differentiate them as the best in the marketplace. The question every person should ask is, 'How can I make myself the best to maximise my chances of gainful and satisfying employment?' This book addresses that issue.

About the author

Dr David Freemantle is the author of 15 books and this, his sixteenth, is based on a lifetime of experiences including a few years on the board of British Caledonian Airways. Born in Southampton, UK, he is a well-known speaker, respected across the world for his seminars on customer service, motivation and leadership. He lives in Makati City, Philippines and works extensively in China and Asia. He can be contacted at *david.freemantle@gmail.com*.

Introduction

This book is for people who want to perform well in their jobs, progress their careers and become the person every organisation wants. It is also for unemployed people currently looking for a job.

From start to finish in your career you will be the chosen one for the simple reason that you have chosen to get that job, whether you are the chief executive of a large organisation or the new graduate trainee in a prestigious company.

Your appointment, whatever it is, will be *your* choice – not the choice of the selection panel delegated the task of filling a vacancy. You will become so 'wanted' by an organisation that they will have no option but to appoint you as opposed to the other candidates whose 'best' is 'second best' compared to the excellence you demonstrate. Such excellence is within reach of everyone who reads this book, whether they be 15 or 65 years old. There are no boundaries in ambition except the physical limitations brought about by age.

Career success is not just about successful interviews and the answers you provide in 45 minutes of questioning. More important are the choices you make during the years preceding each interview. These are the choices you make day by day in your current work – or the choices you make in trying to get work or the choices you make in pursuing promotion or whatever you want. These day-by-day choices will, over the long term, influence your approach at those critical moments of the selection process as well as when performing your current job. This book is about those choices.

Anyone desirous of moving their work situation (or non-work situation) forward from the status quo will benefit from the practical tips expressed in these chapters. You could be a young college graduate aiming for that dream job, or a middle-aged manager desperate to extricate yourself from a rut, or a senior manager aiming for an appointment on the board. You could be a self-employed business person seeking to win a major contract, or a sales representative pitching for your first big-ticket sale. Or you could have just been made redundant after 20 years with a company that went out of business yesterday. You could be jobless in a tough recessionary marketplace where few jobs are available.

The principles and practices expounded here will apply to all. They relate to the 'extras' you provide over and above the 'core' professional skills and knowledge which, for the purpose of this book, it will be taken for granted you have.

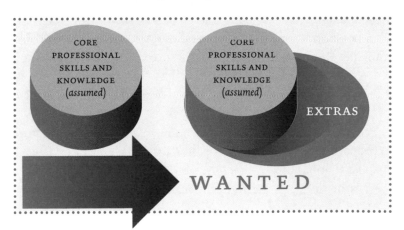

This is my sixteenth book and it is based on 45 years of varying experiences and achievements. This has included the publication of 15 books and a career that saw me leap from the world of science to that of management. My career progression (phase one) resulted in my appointment to the board of an airline at the tender age of 39. I then embarked on a second career pursuing my love of writing, teaching and travelling. Officially retired, I now work harder than ever.

A NOTE ON THE WRITING OF THIS BOOK

The book you have in your hands comprises 50 short chapters and it is recommended that you dip into these at random. It is not necessary to read the book in the conventional way, starting with Chapter 1.

My approach to writing the book was to scribble down each main idea as it came into my head, thus creating a random list of chapter headings. I would then pluck any number from the list, apply my mind to the topic and draft the chapter, next assembling them in a very loose order – in other words the chapters were not written in the order you see them now.

The natural desire in any quest for success is to learn from a rational step-by-step approach. I do not offer this because in my view it is unrealistic. There is and can be no formula for success. This book offers various facets and perspectives, some linked, some not. It is not a comprehensive textbook of knowledge but more a set of stimuli to prompt readers to think about what is wanted by any organisation and how to appeal to those 'wants'.

I have tried to steer away from the conventional stuff about how to prepare an immaculate CV or how to succeed at interviews. I suspect that has already been written about. I make no apology for a rather iconoclastic and provocative approach to becoming WANTED.

I

FALL IN LOVE

Falling in love with your work is potentially less perilous and more rewarding than falling in love with the person of your dreams

Search your heart to discover the type of work you love – and then focus your time and energies on securing that work. Your love for this work will drive you towards it and ensure you perform effectively.

When you love the work you do your bosses (and customers) will love it too.

To make any progress in your job and career you have to fall in love with the work you do. If you love gardening then become a gardener. If you love baking then become a pastry chef. If you love computers then become an expert in information technology.

Wherever you look for successful people you will find people who love what they do

In an interview in the *Daily Telegraph* (20 July 2008) Linda Bennett, founder of the fashion retailer L.K. Bennett, said: 'I have been passionate about shoes since I was a child and I realised early on that you're much more likely to make a success of something if you love what you're doing.'

Nanz Chong-Komo, woman entrepreneur of the year in Singapore in 2000 and winner of the Singapore International Management Action Award in 2001, was founder of the former ONE.99 chain of retail stores. When I interviewed her on 12 July 2002 she stated, 'I don't do this work for money, I do it for love.'

I have yet to find a person who is good at their work who does not love what they do, whether it be tailoring, hairdressing, dentistry or cleaning streets. A few years ago an acquaintance told me of a street-cleaner in London who won an award for service to the community. 'This woman loved what she did,' he said. 'She loved to have the cleanest streets in London. She loved to help passers-by by giving them directions.' Work is all about love. I have even had a funeral director tell me he loved his work.

In his Commencement Address to students of Stanford University on 12 June 2005 the co-founder and CEO of Apple Computers, Steve Jobs, said: 'You've got to find the job you love.'

There is nothing worse than finding people who hate what they do. You will see them in any major city, standing around ignoring customers, not interested in the product and with only one aim in life – to earn money.

If that's your aim, just to earn money, then that's what you will do. But it won't take you too far in your career. To make progress you have to go beyond your wage, salary or fees and fall in love with the business you are in. That means loving to serve customers (internal or external), loving the products you are making or selling and loving to expend physical, mental and emotional energies on these activities.

Just as people fall out of love with each other some employees fall out of love with their jobs mid-career – and change direction, falling in love with a new type of work. A typical story is of a 30-year-old woman who, having had a successful career in advertising, gradually fell out of love with it, resigned and embarked on a career in acupuncture and yoga. The money was less, the hard work the same, but the happiness much greater.

Loving your work does not come with a price. There is no correlation between salary and the amount of love you feel for your work. In fact as you pursue higher levels of income the risk is that your love turns to greed. This was the case with some unscrupulous bankers and the sub-prime crisis, the precursor to the September 2008 global financial crash.

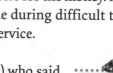

Work is
love made visible

Few people embark on nursing careers for the money. Most do so because they love caring for people during difficult times. The same applies to any type of social service.

It was Kahlil Gibran (in *The Prophet*) who said, 'Work is love made visible'. Summarily it is far better earning 10 thousand doing work you love than 20 thousand doing work you hate. The extra money will never bring you the happiness that can be attained when you love your work.

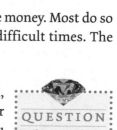

QUESTION
What work do
you love
doing most?

PRACTICAL TIPS

Rewrite the following using yourself and two friends as examples:

- Reubens fell in love with graphic design and is now a leading designer in his company.
- Katharine loves child-care and now runs her own nursery for under-fives.
- Sophie loves the challenge of fixing problems for customers and won an award last year for service excellence.

2

BELIEVE YOU
CAN DO IT

Belief is the essence of success

No matter how many setbacks you experience in pursuing your career goals you have to believe that one day you will achieve them. If you lose belief you will give up and become defeated. Belief is an essential motivational driver in your career. You have to believe this!

One of my favourite quotations is by the French Nobel Literature laureate Anatole France: 'To accomplish great things we must not only act, but also dream, not only plan but also believe.' This statement has been a driving force in my life.

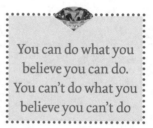

You can do what you believe you can do. You can't do what you believe you can't do

Here are two of my own personal examples: 'I dreamed I would travel the world and visit many countries. I believed I could. I did so.' 'I dreamed I would write a book and get it published. I believed I could. I did so.'

Back in 1859 nobody believed it was possible to get a man on the moon. Just over 100 years later, speaking to a Joint Session of Congress on 25 May 1961, President John F. Kennedy declared: 'I believe that this nation should commit itself to achieve the goal, before this decade is out, of landing a man on the moon and returning him safely to the earth. No single space project in this period will be more impressive to mankind.'

That goal was achieved on 21 July 1969 when the first person set foot on the lunar surface. 'That's one small step for man, one giant leap for mankind,' said Neil Armstrong.

You are more likely to fail in the absence of belief than if you have it. So whatever your goals in life you have to believe you can achieve them. First it means (in the context of this book) focusing on your career goals as well as those for your current job. Second, it means digging deep into your soul to discover whether you really do have the belief that you can achieve these goals.

Another way of looking at this is as follows: 'If someone else can achieve it then I believe I can too.' This is applicable whether your goal is to run a Fortune 500 company or devote your life to reducing poverty. It does not matter whether your goals are long term or short term as long as you believe you can achieve them. This belief emanates from the soul and relates to what is really important to you in the future.

Whilst the essential motivational drivers are dreams and beliefs it is important to differentiate these from fantasies. The prospect of any fantasy coming true is remote. I might have a fantasy of winning a few million on the lottery, but in 14 years I did not win more than £100 on any one occasion, despite an outlay during this period of many thousands. Equally I might have a fantasy of meeting a beautiful young starlet and living with her in paradise on some exotic tropical island with palm trees, white beaches and crystal-clear blue water. Both fantasies are unrealistic. To make a dream come true you must have a belief that it can come true, a belief that the dream can be converted into a future practical reality.

Furthermore you can only turn a dream into reality if you believe there is specific action you can take, no matter how tough, that will lead you in that direction. There is no action I can take to realise a fantasy. Even if I spent a million buying lottery tickets the probability of winning more than a million is very low. However, I can take action to write a book and get it published. Belief relates to what you 'can do' and not to what you 'can't do', and most people can do much more than they think. Thus belief requires the removal of mental barriers such as defeatism and negativity.

With genuine belief anything that is realistically possible can be made to happen. If you are currently jobless you have to believe that 'out there' is the perfect job waiting for you... and that you can do something about getting it. If you are seeking promotion and have already been passed over twice you have to believe that eventually you will be elevated into a position you prize. But first you have to believe you can do something about gaining that promotion.

To quote Martti Ahtisaari (2008 Nobel Peace laureate): 'You have to listen, learn and believe in unimagined solutions to seemingly intractable problems.'

PRACTICAL TIPS

- Long-term motivational drives come from dreams and beliefs. The only way to develop these is to dig deeply into your heart and soul and examine clearly the forces driving your life (and your work).
- Be brutally honest in identifying these forces.
- Then, when it comes to your work and career, focus on unleashing these personal forces.
- Use these powerful forces (the motivational drivers) to generate the energies for realising the goals you believe you can achieve.
- You have to convince yourself that everything is possible.

3

DELIVER
RESULTS

If you don't know what results are required of you, you stand no chance

Always keep focused on your company's goals, and then work backwards from there to determine the results you have to achieve on a day-by-day basis.

This is at the crux of employment. For any work there must be an end result that is of value to employers and their customers. There is no point in labouring away unless it helps bring in the money. The expenditure of your physical, emotional and intellectual energies will be in vain if nothing happens which benefits your company. That beneficial result might be a sale, a problem fixed, a positive customer experience, a deadline met or a financial target achieved. Every employee should be clear about the results expected of them and how these contribute to the overall performance of the company.

Every day keep a picture in your mind of the results required of you

This means an effective response to the question: 'What am I here for?' The answer is not, 'I am here to please my boss' or 'I am here to earn money'. Nor is it 'I am here to carry out the tasks I'm told to do'. The answer is 'I am here to deliver results linked to the company's goals'. Every employee needs to be clear about this link.

Too many organisations are task driven. The focus is on the task rather than on what the task should achieve. Tasks are the same as assigned activities, directed actions or instructions. An example is stacking shelves rather than attending to a customer waiting to be served. In such cases employees and their bosses lose sight of the end result – to maximise sales by creating an incredibly positive experience for a customer. Keeping a customer hanging around is not conducive to this.

When people are clear about the results expected of them and how these link to company goals they will be able to determine their daily tasks accordingly. This is called empowerment. In the absence of empowerment there is 'command and control' and all people do is what their bosses tell them to do.

Successful people are highly focused on results. They will 'read' the business well and even generate their own objectives if the organisation is so muddled it fails to specify the goals to be achieved. The people who are thus wanted are those who can see clearly what has to be achieved and also how to go about it. The 'how' is the task. The 'what' is an individual result essentially linked to a corporate goal.

The advantage of being results oriented is that you are more likely to achieve meaningful results than if you are task oriented. When asked at the interview, 'What have you done over the last few years?' it is far better to say, 'I have contributed to increased sales by consistently achieving a 93 per cent customer satisfaction rating' than 'I have answered 80 calls a day'.

Any organisation will want people who achieve results linked to goals. All you have to do is convince them (as well as yourself) that you deliver great results.

PRACTICAL TIPS
- Stop saying 'I do this at work' and instead say 'This is what I achieve at work, day by day'.
- Stop seeing work as tasks but instead see it as a set of important results to be achieved.
- Create your own qualitative and quantitative measures for gauging these results.
- Establish a clear link in your mind between how the results you have to achieve are linked to corporate goals.

4

BE 100 PER CENT TRUSTWORTHY EVERY DAY

Trust is at the core of all relationships

A key driver in your everyday work should be trust (and thus never doing anything to betray this trust). Aim to become the person everyone trusts.

The question you should challenge yourself daily with is, 'Can I be trusted?' For example, 'Can I be trusted to return that telephone call I promised for this morning?' or 'Can I be trusted to lend support to a colleague buckling under pressure?'

Trust is applicable to our daily behaviours as well as the way companies go about their business in the long term. Trust arises when there is openness, honesty and integrity as well as fairness. It can be applied to any business transaction and to all the relationships necessary for this.

If bankers speculate with your precious cash deposits then there is a betrayal of trust. Thus the speculators who turned the country of Iceland into a virtual gigantic hedge fund and who nearly bankrupted Iceland's economy in October 2008 betrayed trust, as did the 'professional financial advisers' who advised many local authorities in the UK to invest funds in Icelandic financial institutions.

Another example is the '2008 melamine scandal' in China when it was discovered that certain food manufacturers were contaminating milk products with the toxic material melamine. Babies died as a result and thousands suffered from kidney stones. This was a betrayal of trust.

These are major examples. The minor examples relating to everyday behaviour are equally important. Can you be trusted to reply to an email on time? Can you be trusted to achieve what you have committed to achieve? Can you be trusted to tell the truth and not cover up your mistakes? Can you be trusted to pay back money you have borrowed? There are a million other examples.

The people wanted in any organisation are those who are 100 per cent trustworthy. It implies that the senior executives can equally be trusted (and of course there is much evidence that some senior executives cannot be trusted – the Enron scandal of 2001 provides an example, as does the recent Bernard Madoff fiasco).

Professor Donald Sull of London Business School asserts that to 'make it happen' you must have employees who are prepared to make commitments (or promises) and who can be trusted to keep these.

In the development of any career it is essential that you aim to develop a reputation for being completely trustworthy. This can only be gained if your everyday behaviours comply with this value (of trust), no matter how it is interpreted by your colleagues.

PRACTICAL TIPS

- To act in a trustworthy way you need to trust yourself. This means creating personal disciplines (such as follow-up methods) which ensure that everything you say and do is compliant with trustworthiness.
- It also requires you to be ruthlessly self-critical in your dealings with everyone to ensure you honour all your commitments.

5

THE
IMPORTANCE OF
IMPORTANCE

It is important that everything you think, say and do reflects what is important to you

This subject is so important that you must question yourself daily on what influences your decisions and communication.

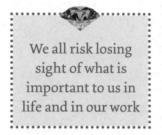

We all risk losing sight of what is important to us in life and in our work

People who are clear about what is important to them will not only be more impressive but go further in their lives and careers. President Barack Obama is a great example. He is so clear about what is important to him and the people of the USA.

It is easy to determine when individuals are speaking about matters important to them: they are convincing and exhibit confidence. When people know what is important to them it influences their decision making and communication.

The choice of what is important to you can only be yours. Nobody (including your employer) can instruct you on this. However it is impossible for everything to be important to you. Conversely it is impossible that nothing is important to you. The width of the 'spectrum of importance' is infinite. You must position yourself accordingly in balancing one important thing against another – for example, is time with your family more or less important to you than working every available waking hour to earn a high salary? In fact how you spend your time is a reflection of what is important to you.

Another challenge relates to expediency. Cutting corners and breaking rules, even at the behest of your boss, are examples.

Choosing between the safest route and the riskiest one is another reflection on what you consider important.

What is important to you is synonymous with your values. There are too many misunderstandings about values. Thus in annual reports you will often find statements of 'company values'. Companies do not exist other than as legal entities in the world of commerce. Companies cannot have values. Only people can have values.

During our upbringing we are all inculcated with a set of values held dear by our parents and our teachers. They instruct us, for example, that 'good manners' are important, and thus most of us are brought up to believe this too. However the reading of biographies will quickly lead one to the conclusion that the breadth of values important to us is very wide. As adults it behoves us to challenge all these values and work out for ourselves what is really important, especially when it comes to our jobs and careers. When you are very clear about this and can articulate it well you will be wanted, especially by those who also consider this important.

PRACTICAL TIP

- Discuss this chapter with your colleagues at work and also with your family. See if you can obtain a consensus of what is important to all of you when it comes to your work. The discussion will lead to a greater clarity of purpose on your part.

6

GO MAD

All successful people go MAD. They go and make a difference

Ensure that the contribution you make every day at work makes a difference to the people that count (your customers, your colleagues, your boss, etc.).

When you are the same as everyone else nobody will notice you and the probability of you being chosen will be based on random selection.

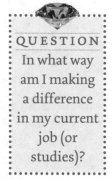

QUESTION
In what way am I making a difference in my current job (or studies)?

Given the premise that every human being is unique it should not be too difficult to make a difference. But even so, many struggle to differentiate themselves from others. Should there be six short-list candidates you cannot afford to be the same as the other five – you will need some differentiating experiences, achievements and characteristics that set you apart from the 'run-of-the-mill' crowd of applicants.

In everything you say or do there is an opportunity to differentiate and develop your own unique approach. This effectively becomes your USP (unique selling point). For example, you can make a difference through your ...

... unique professional expertise
... unique relationship skills
... unique personality
... unique experience in a specific industry
... unique ability to motivate team members
... unique track record for getting results.

The challenge throughout your career is to develop a distinctive track record that sets you apart from those in the crowded centres of convention. You will need to develop and know the key factors that distinguish you and which enhance your prospects of selection when the crucial moment of truth arises.

In preparing to make a difference you should ask yourself these essential questions: 'In what way am I making a difference in my current job (or studies)?' 'In what way did I make a difference in my previous jobs?'

Patricia Halaguena, a senior flight attendant with Philippine Airlines, says, 'Even when I'm busy I make time to talk to customers, knowing that this makes them feel important'. She is so different from flight attendants on many other airlines who simply go through the motions, following their routines to the letter of the rule book. Making a difference is about going beyond the routine and the immediate task in hand.

Here are further examples ...
... you have a unique ability of winning over customers who have been alienated
... you have a unique ability for addressing and resolving major quality issues
... you have unique experience of putting stressed clients at their ease
... you have a unique talent for installing complex software
... you have a unique way of getting things done quickly
... the exceptionally high quality of your work is unique
... you are unique in the way you size up a problem quickly and identify the root cause.

When you are the same as everyone else few people will remember you. You become memorable by the characteristics and contribution by which you differentiate yourself.

Given that we live in a world where many are notoriously unreliable, for example failing to deliver on promises, some successful people simply make a difference by being 100 per cent reliable. They deliver what they say they are going to deliver. They never let anyone down. They become completely trustworthy in a society where many cannot be trusted to convert fine words into action.

The key thing about going MAD (going to **Make A Difference**) is that little things can make a big difference. In the world of commerce customers tend to take the big things for granted but often judge you by the little things.

A few years ago I went through a divorce. I needed a lawyer to help me. In the UK it is accepted legal practice that you can have an initial non-chargeable half-hour meeting with a lawyer before committing to engage him or her. So I decided to meet six different lawyers before choosing one to represent my interests. Two of the lawyers were immediately eliminated from my list because no one answered the phone when I called to make an appointment. Little things make a big difference. Of the remaining four lawyers one kept looking at his watch during our half-hour meeting. A second did all the talking without taking any interest in my individual circumstances. A third demanded my ID and proof of address before I was allowed to enter his office. The fourth, who I engaged, sat me down, offered me refreshments and listened intently to what I had to say.

Little things make a big difference. If you are a lawyer reading this I recommend that you go MAD and offer your client a cup of tea! (Only one out of four did in my case.)

PRACTICAL TIPS

- Focus on developing your own 'unique selling proposition'.

Rewrite the following using yourself as an example:

- 'As an operations manager I made a difference by improving operational efficiency and reducing costs.'
- 'When I took over as Team Leader morale was low. I made a difference by putting a lot of emphasis on team building to raise morale.'
- 'As a graduate trainee I made a difference by successfully completing a challenging project to eliminate the glitches on our new system.'

Career stimuli 1

DRIVERS

- The journey is yours.
- The job you are in is yours.
- The career you have is yours.
- Your future is yours alone.
- Wherever you want to go you have to drive there yourself.
- You cannot be a passenger.
- Nobody else can take you where you want to go.
- Motivation is your driver.
- And where you should be going is where you will be WANTED.

7

GO DOWN THE ROAD LESS TRAVELLED

Two roads diverged in a wood, and I –
I took the one less traveled by,
And that has made all the difference.

The Road Not Taken, Robert Frost (1916)

In tackling anything avoid choosing the well-trodden paths that everyone else has gone down. The differential comes when you create your own path or choose a path less well trodden.

Every minute, every day and throughout your life awake you will be making choices. Most of those choices will be simple, for example whether to say 'Yes' or 'No' or when to take exercise (if at all). Choice can relate to

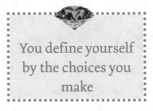

You define yourself by the choices you make

everything you do, say and even think (assuming you are conscious). It can relate to the food you eat, the newspapers you read and what programmes to watch on television. Furthermore and most essentially, the choices you make have a phenomenal impact on your career. These choices differentiate you, especially when you choose the road less travelled.

For a skier this would mean going 'off-piste'. For a tourist it would mean exploring an ancient city yourself rather than sitting atop the conventional tour bus and being informed by the typical multilingual guide.

Such adventure will broaden your mind, spark creativity, demand intellectual vigour and show you are willing to take risks. It will mean avoiding convention and venturing into unknown territory.

Most people avoid the unfamiliar. They follow the herd and go down the road 'most travelled'. They get into a habit or routine, effectively behaving mechanistically without a moment's thought. Robots do not make choices. They are programmed to respond in a certain way. We humans risk doing the same. We allow ourselves subconsciously to become programmed like a robot and travel down pre-programmed paths.

In the absence of such conscious choice life becomes easy. The risk appears low and the energy required minimal. If you want a journey through your comfort zones then you will take the road most travelled. Along these highways there is minimal risk and minimal choice because there is minimal demand on your intellectual energies. But such routes will rarely lead you to the job you want, let alone provide the career you desire. There is no easy route. I love the challenge of 'Do I turn left or right?' when there is no clear sign. That's why I, as a British citizen, live in the Philippines.

To make progress in our careers we need to examine closely our choices (small and big) with a view to choosing routes to success that others have not found. It means searching new territories and making new discoveries for the benefit of the team and the organisation. This can apply to any facet of our work and is vital for creative innovation and progress.

In his Commencement Address (see Chapter 1) Steve Jobs tells how he dropped out of college and then chose to take a class in calligraphy. He went down the road less travelled and it made all the difference (to the world of computing as well as to himself). By choosing to study calligraphy he learnt about serif and sans serif typefaces as well as about varying the amount of space between different letter combinations. He learnt about what makes for great typography. As a result of this and ten years later he came up with the idea of putting different fonts into computer text and making screen typefaces beautiful. The Apple Mac, which he invented, was the first computer to have multiple typefaces or proportionally spaced fonts. To quote from his address: 'Your time is limited, so don't waste it living someone else's life. Don't be trapped by dogma – which is living with the results of other people's thinking.'

The singer, the late Eartha Kitt, was once asked to what she attributed her success. She replied, 'I didn't follow the herd, I followed my own path.'

PRACTICAL TIP

- Take a trip to some place you have not previously visited – perhaps a spot in the countryside, or a park you've never set foot in. Then take a long walk and carefully consider the roads less travelled in your life: past, present and future. (You're on such a road at the moment.) With a fresh mind review the choices you make – for example to become wanted by others.

8

PUT YOUR
JOB INTO 3-D

All jobs have three dimensions. It is not sufficient to confine yourself to the first dimension only – the tasks in the job description

For maximum success at work you need to be clear about the 'how', the 'what' and the 'why' of your job.

It is tempting to assert that job descriptions are a waste of time, but perhaps more realistic to say they provide a summary sketch of the tasks your boss has in mind for your job. Most job descriptions I have seen are boring and elicit zero motivational response.

A '3-D' approach to your work will bring your job to life and enhance your career prospects

All jobs are three dimensional:

1 DIMENSION 1 – the elements of the job as described. These are the tasks you need to undertake. They represent the basic *'how?'* of your job.
2 DIMENSION 2 – the results you have to achieve day by day. This is the measurable contribution you make as a result of your efforts. It represents the essential *'what?'* of your job.
3 DIMENSION 3 – the overall purpose of your job. This is the link to company goals and should be a key motivational force. It represents the fundamental *'why?'* of your job.

Most job descriptions merely describe 'Dimension 1' – the tasks to be undertaken. Such task orientation is not enough. It turns employees into robots.

There is no point kicking a ball ('Dimension 1') unless you aim to score or prevent a goal ('Dimension 2') and thus help your team win the game and eventually the league ('Dimension 3').

Successful people do not just undertake tasks assigned to them but frame in their minds the three-dimensional contributions necessary for ensuring the future success of the company. Using this '3-D' approach they gradually develop their approach to accomplish this. In this way the job evolves through a series of small changes.

For example, many restaurant managers will hire waiters and waitresses to carry out the tasks (as per the job description) of cleaning tables, taking orders, delivering meals to the table and collecting payment before a party of diners leave. This is a singular approach with a sole focus on the task. As such there is little scope for change. You may as well have self-serve microwaves in a restaurant and get customers to push button 37 for hot chicken and rice. The technology is available to carry out these uni-dimensional tasks without the intervention of waiters.

The best restaurant managers go beyond the one-dimensional task approach. Applying '3-D' they aim for every diner to leave the restaurant having enjoyed an incredibly positive experience. To achieve this these managers give waiters and waitresses maximum freedom to develop their job such that every customer is totally happy. With such positive outcomes diners return time and time again. Thus I have encountered at various times waiters who have evolved their at-table-service to include magic, comedy, stage acting, dancing, therapy (advice), being a sounding board (listening) as well as offering instruction in how to prepare a dish.

To give just one example: in Penang, Malaysia I was looking for a restaurant in which to have dinner. As often happens in Asia there was a waitress standing outside each restaurant with a menu in hand, trying to lure customers inside. One such waitress caught my eye and smiled. Her name was Ni Ni. 'You look like a fishman,' Ni Ni exclaimed. 'Excuse me?' came my startled reply, not quite understanding. 'You look like a man who loves fish!' she explained. I confirmed that I did and she then informed me they had some wonderfully fresh fish on the menu that evening. With her '3-D' approach Ni Ni effectively sold me a positive dining experience. She guided me inside and introduced me to Chan Leong Pim, my waiter for the evening. He made pure theatre out of placing the napkin on my lap. He unfolded the napkin with a flourish, and waved it around above his head as if it was a flag before deftly spreading it on to my lap. Most waiters just place the napkin on your lap (the 'Dimension 1' task). Some waiters don't even do that. You do it yourself. What Ni Ni and Chan Leong Pim had done was evolve their jobs into an enjoyable form of theatrical service. Their restaurant got my business that evening.

This is an example of the three-dimensional approach to developing a job:

1 DIMENSION 1 – the task of serving a meal (the basic *how* you go about your job).
2 DIMENSION 2 – focusing on *what* has to be achieved day by day (for each customer a positive dining experience with theatrical flourishes).
3 DIMENSION 3 – being clear about *why* this has to be achieved (happy customers bring more business).

When employees are solely task oriented and robotic they stop thinking about what they do. They cease to be imaginative. They lose sight of the desirable outcomes. This is dangerous. However, as soon as you start thinking about your job and how to do it better you initiate the process of applying a '3-D' approach.

In other words to fulfil your ambitions and maximise your contribution you have to go beyond the job 'as described'. When you accomplish this you will be much wanted for the simple reason that you will attract more business or improve the efficiency of it.

PRACTICAL TIPS

- Every so often ask yourself these important questions:
    'What is my work all about?'
    'What am I doing here?'
    'Why am I here?'
    'How can I go about making things even better?'
- Relate these to the three dimensions stated above and consistently answer the *how*, *what* and *why* questions about your work. Then use your imagination (in '3-D' mode) in evolving your job into something better for all.

Career stimuli 2

DIFFERENTIALS

- When everyone is the same the choice is random.
- Do not be the same as everyone else.
- It is you who create the difference.
- It is the little things that make a big difference.
- Everything you do and say can make a difference.
- The determining factors will be the differences you create.
- When you can convince people that you can make a bigger difference to the organisation than anyone else then you will be WANTED.

9

RESONATE

When you touch a person's heart and soul you resonate

To commit to a genuine agreement you need to reach into your heart and seek to resonate with the other person.

There is a tendency, especially in the USA, to use the phrase 'What you say resonates with me' as opposed to 'I agree with what you say'. There is an important distinction. Agreement is the result of a rational thought process and signifies the acceptance of ideas or opinions proffered by another person. Resonance (in the psychological context) goes beyond this to include emotional harmony. There is also a spiritual component. The statement 'What you say resonates with me' indicates the twanging of an emotional chord and feeling reflected in the statement: 'This person is talking the same language as me, she is on my wavelength.'

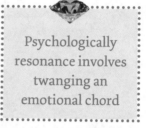

Psychologically resonance involves twanging an emotional chord

In this context a related word is 'accord'. When you reach an accord it implies there is harmony and unity. There is an emotional as well as spiritual element to an accord. Resonance occurs when you touch a chord and this is reflected back through an echo. The main difference between an accord and resonance is that the former tends to be 'formal' whilst the latter is more an informal and spontaneous process.

Dissonance occurs when no positive emotional chord is struck. The words expressed grate and negative feelings are generated. Dissonance has the same relationship to discord and disagreement as resonance has to accord and agreement.

In practice to resonate means tuning into another person's wavelength to connect not just with her thoughts (as expressed in what she says) but also with the emotions that underpin these. When there is clarity, balance and an echo in the two-way transmission of ideas and feelings in all probability there will be a mutually beneficial understanding and harmony. This is resonance. The two sounds become one. This is unity. 'We speak the same language', 'We are on the same wavelength'.

To become wanted in any organisation requires such resonance. It requires developing the skill, when walking into a room of strangers, to tune in quickly to their wavelength and reflect back clearly that you are also on the same wavelength. This will endear you to them and spark a reaction, 'This person is like one of us'. They will sense the harmony that can be achieved in working with you for the simple reason that what you say, and the way you say it, touches emotional chords with them (and vice versa).

People who have superb relationship skills have this innate ability to resonate with others. But even if it is not in your genes you can develop the skill by sensitising yourself to the reactions of others and your reactions to them. You can practise by focusing on all the little signals people send out and trying to understand their underlying meaning. You can then respond effectively. For example, would you a trust a person whose eyes shift around frequently and who does not look at you whilst you speak? How would you react to a person who has a persistent smirk on his face? Shifting eyes and smirks are barriers to resonance and you need to develop your sensitivity to these minutiae of human behaviour. They tell you a lot.

These aspects of body language reflect the emotional undertones that colour people's behaviour (together with the spiritual forces that drive it) and if you fail to sensitise yourself to them then you stand little chance of resonating with others and becoming wanted.

··

PRACTICAL TIP

- When in serious discussion with a colleague or a boss ask yourself, 'Does what she is saying resonate with me?' If the answer is 'Yes' you are more likely to reach agreement than if the answer is 'No'.

··

10
BE YOURSELF

To be yourself in any organisation is far more challenging than being what the organisation wants you to be. Conscience often conflicts with conformity

Reflect on what you want to be in life and at work – and then focus your mind on becoming that person.

When you try to be what someone else wants you to be you become a ventriloquist's dummy and the proverbial 'yes-man' who appeases to please his strong-arm bosses. In doing so you will lose your sense of self together with the respect of wise people who will see you for what you are: nobody worth listening to.

Careers are built on an increasing sense of self-worth in which you value your 'self' and what you have to offer. To achieve this requires evolving your own set of principles and beliefs to be used as a foundation for decision making – no matter how those decisions grate with your seniors. This is at the core of what you are as a human being.

One client of mine, the head of human resources of a major subsidiary of a large conglomerate, tells how she could not, on principle, acquiesce to her chief executive's proposed pay policy. So she informed him she was going to take the issue to the group president as she felt the proposed policy would conflict with everything she stood for in rewarding employees. She did so. It was a high-risk strategy. The group president listened carefully to her,

In being true to yourself you will need to develop a high degree of self-awareness

agreed with her, and the subsidiary's chief executive was removed from the job.

In being true to yourself you will need to develop a high degree of self-awareness and a clear idea of what you want to be in life. This does not only relate to ambition ('I want to be a successful musician') but also to principles ('I want to be open and transparent') and, equally important, to behaviour ('I always want to be punctual').

You cannot be everything in life, nor can you be nothing. As alluded to in Chapter 5, in between are an infinite number of possibilities. Only you can decide what you want to be (in every sense) and only then do you stand any chance of making progress in your career.

If you don't know what you want to be in life then there is little possibility you will become anybody worth respecting – and few people will want you.

Here is an example of what someone wants to be: 'I want to be a highly respected head teacher who is easy to get along with. I want to be inspirational, progressive and professional. I want to be punctual. I want to be positive. I want to be a person who is open to suggestions and a good listener. I want to be a person who demonstrates respect for all no matter what their background and current circumstances. I want to be proactive in implementing improvement at our school. Overall I want our students to benefit from the education we provide so their chance of success in life is enhanced. This is the core of what I want to be professionally.'

PRACTICAL TIPS

Specify how you want to develop your character and the future contribution you intend to make. For example:

Character development:

- I want to be a person who is quietly confident but introspective, or:
- I want to be a person who is charming and outgoing.

Future contribution:

- I want to be head of sales and marketing in a major company, or:
- I want to be known for my charitable work for the homeless.

Rewrite these stating what you want to be. Use the above example as a template.

Career stimuli ③

CORE

- The core is you.
- You have a large soft core that you can change.
- Embedded within is a small hard core that you cannot change.
- The core is your spirit, your soul, your heart and your intellect.
- The core is your principles, beliefs and values.
- The core is your character, personality and genetic make-up.
- It is the core that generates the differentials.
- It is the core that drives an individual.
- It is the core that creates original ideas.
- You need to unlock, expose and develop the core that is 'you'.
- Identification and expression of the core will determine whether or not you are WANTED.

II

HAVE STRONG
CONVICTIONS

Your conscience is a critical guide to your daily conduct at work

When alarm bells ring in your conscience always take note and take action. Do not hide from your conscience – it reflects the essence of what you are all about as a human being. Consult it daily. At work – as well as at home – become a man (or woman) who couples conviction with reality.

During their lives most people will face a dilemma: do I make a stand on principle or do I acquiesce and be expedient? This is particularly important at work, where bosses sometimes ask people to do things against their will. In the ideal organisation everyone would share the

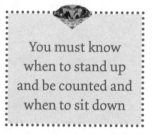

You must know when to stand up and be counted and when to sit down

same convictions and such conflicts of conscience would be avoided. But this is rarely the case, mainly because people's practical interpretation of principles varies widely. Thus many people assert they are candid and trustworthy whilst behaving in ways that are the antithesis of these principles.

Martti Ahtisaari, 2008 Nobel Peace laureate said: 'Some of the people I have dealt with are now senior people in their country's government. They used to call themselves "freedom-fighters" whilst others called them "terrorists". When you negotiate you can't always stand on principle. You don't negotiate with Sunday school teachers.'

Convictions, which comprise a *mélange* of personally held principles, values, beliefs and opinions are such abstract concepts that their conversion into daily conduct can often be disputed. The obvious examples are presidents who propel their country into war yet declare themselves devoutly religious (and thus presumably adherents of the non-violent principles most religions advocate). The reality of this world is that to make progress people often have to set aside their principles. The critical issue is 'When?'

The principles that drive our daily lives are developed internally within our souls and can never be imposed externally by preaching, no matter how evangelical. At best there can be external influence, but never imposition. Equally expediency and the abandonment of principles can never be imposed upon us. It is always our decision.

When deciding between 'taking a stand' and 'expediency' we have to separate the strong convictions (upon which we will make a stand) from those whose hold on our conscience is weak – thus permitting a degree of expediency.

We will have to make decisions such as:

1 Is this an issue on which I will resign on principle?
2 Is this an issue I feel so strongly about that I have to confront my boss on it?
3 Is this an issue that is not sufficiently important to me that I can acquiesce?
4 Will I impede progress by standing on principle or should I be expedient, set my principles aside, and achieve what everyone wants me to achieve?

These issues might relate to safety, financial compliance, the treatment of employees, our relationships with customers or resolving an intractable problem (say between unions and employers). Suffice it to say that people who are always expedient will be perceived as having no backbone, a weak character and as invariably blowing with the wind. Conversely the zealots who fight every corner on principle will alienate the majority. The line between the two extremes can only be drawn by each one of us and it will take courage to stand by it.

A good employer will not want a 'yes-man'

The person who is wanted in any organisation is one who is seen to have both strong convictions for which she is prepared to fight whilst on lesser issues she is prepared to be flexible and compromise.

It is worth concluding with something said by Ingrid Betancourt, who was held hostage by FARC rebels in the Colombian jungle and released after six years: 'During my six years of captivity I learnt a lot about human nature. I had little else to do but observe my guards closely. I learnt how weak people can be under group pressure. People become so afraid that they will say and do the opposite to what they feel and think.'

PRACTICAL TIPS

- On a regular basis review the core principles that you hold dear when it comes to work and challenge yourself: 'Do I apply these principles in my everyday decisions and actions?'
- Ask yourself: 'Am I a person respected for the strength of my convictions at work?'
- Also ask yourself: 'Am I strong enough to take a stand on principle?'

12

EMBRACE
MUTUALITY

For the good of yourself be good to others. This is mutuality

At the core of any relationship is mutual respect, mutual support and mutual trust. Embrace this in all aspects of your work and career. Conversely, avoid working with people who cannot reciprocate.

We are born selfish, screaming aloud as we make huge demands on our parents. For some there is never any appreciation of such support and we remain selfish throughout our lives, only interested in ourselves and manipulating others to meet our needs. These are the people who 'take'

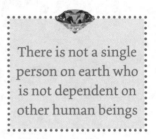

There is not a single person on earth who is not dependent on other human beings

rather than 'give', who would rather talk about themselves than find out about you. The world is full of such egotists and suffers accordingly.

Organisations also suffer as such egotists foment internal politics and power plays become rife. If that is the game you want to play then this book is not for you. Conversely if you believe that ethics and morality have a role in modern-day working practice then you will find that 'mutuality' is at the core of that approach. When a company prides itself on its integrity there will be an emphasis on mutual trust, mutual respect, mutual support and mutual care in all relationships, whether they be with customers, employees, suppliers, managers, shareholders or the surrounding community. There will be a fine understanding of the 'give and take' equilibrium such that no one is taken advantage of and the benefits of trade are divided fairly in a mutually acceptable way.

Mutuality should be a personal philosophy whereby you avoid exploiting the weak and, just to err on the side of a clear conscience, you give more than you take. Every single person on earth wants to be respected for something or other. Mutuality means seeking out and demonstrating those aspects of an individual you can respect and showing that respect. In this way the other person will respect you too. Mutuality also means providing support to those who are prepared to support you. Trust is an equally important component. Mutuality is when you demonstrate you trust a person at the same time as having the confidence that he or she trusts you.

Mutuality creates an equilibrium by which a relationship can thrive. When that relationship is infected by disrespect, mistrust, lack of support and care then an imbalance occurs which risks severe alienation and becoming 'unwanted'.

The initiative to demonstrate mutuality should always be with you. This means signalling respect, showing trust, providing support and care at the first available opportunity without waiting for the other person to show it first. This is important when approaching an interview or meeting for the first time with a new boss or new employee. No matter what you have heard on the grapevine you should always assume the best and reveal your willingness to support and trust this person and thus indicate your respect for him.

PRACTICAL TIPS

- Forget about yourself and always focus on the other person, discovering things you like about him (or her) along with those traits you can respect. Demonstrate that respect (e.g. 'I'm really impressed with what you achieved in that last sales campaign').

- Always assume you can trust a person. Most times the person will then act in a trustworthy way (e.g. 'I trust you will return this flash-disk to me tomorrow').
- Provide support when asked but not when the other person has failed to support you on the last five occasions.

13

GIVE
SOMETHING
AWAY EVERY DAY

The more you give away the richer you will become

Give something away every day.

Good people get recognised. They are seen to be generous, open, honest and trustworthy. They keep to their word and they give extra whenever they can. These are the people most organisations want.

Personally I live by a code of giving something away every day. I try to be generous without allowing people to take advantage and exploit me. I have always given my clients more than they bargained for. For example I have never charged my clients my full expenses and I have always given them extra time for which I have not charged a fee. I am not like those lawyers or accountants who faithfully record every unit of time (normally five minutes) dedicated to a client and charge accordingly.

I am not completely virtuous and have sinned in many ways, but that is for my autobiography. However when it comes to generosity I think I do pretty well. It just happens to be a philosophy of mine. At lunches with clients I will be the one who calls for the bill rather than one of those miserly people who always holds back, hoping not to pay. This philosophy also extends to giving thanks, giving praise and showing appreciation.

Giving does not just relate to material things and money but more importantly to giving something from your heart. This could be as simple as giving five minutes of your time and a listening ear to an acquaintance with a personal problem.

It is worth concluding this chapter with two stories from the Philippines. The first is from the *Philippine Daily Inquirer* (14

December 2008). It is about Rey Almonidovar, who lives in Manila. He is 52 and since being fired from a printing company has remained unemployed. He survives on a meagre allowance of 1,000 pesos (approximately £14) a month provided by his sister. He goes around collecting discarded scraps of cloth and buttons. Using pins that he purchases with part of his allowance he converts these materials into headbands, on which he prints an appropriate slogan. He carries these to anti-government rallies and distributes the headbands to protesters free of charge. Asked why he didn't try to sell these headbands, given he was so poor, he replied, 'Unlike the greedy politicians and businessmen I want to share the little money I have.'

Even when you have so little you can give something away.

The second story takes me back four years to when I was staying in a hotel in Manila. I went to the nearby minimart late one evening to purchase some juice. As I stepped back on to the street I was greeted by a scraggy, bearded beggar who tried out his limited English on me. So I emptied my pocket of change and gave it to him. This approximated to £1. He was very grateful and saluted me as he quickly stuffed the coins into his ragged trouser pocket. Meanwhile a gang of about ten street kids (who have no homes and live on the streets) saw me giving money away and rushed towards me with outstretched hands. They tugged my trousers and said, 'Mister, mister, mister, money please!' They ignored the elderly beggar still standing by me. I had no coins left and he saw my dilemma. He graciously intervened. Speaking in Tagalog (the national language) he pushed the street kids back, put his hand in his pocket and gave each child one of the coins he had just received from me. This poor beggar was genuine in trying to help beggar children who were worse off than him. His generosity moved me. I learnt a lot from him. I try to give something away every day.

PRACTICAL TIPS

Set yourself this challenge for the following week:

- Give away three things you value.
- Give some money to a deserving person or cause.
- Give away half an hour of your time to someone who needs your help.
- Give some appreciation to someone who is doing a great job.

14

MAKE 'YES' (NOT 'NO') YOUR DEFAULT OPTION

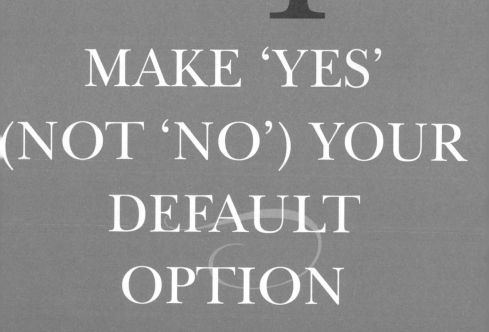

The word 'yes' empowers you. It empowers others

When you request something you want the other person to say 'yes'. So be like that person. Say 'yes' whenever you can. Then everybody will want you.

Saying 'yes' is at the core of positivity. Instinctively we are negative. It is in our genes. As youngsters we are taught boundaries by admonition (for example, 'Don't go near that hot iron').

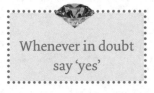

Whenever in doubt say 'yes'

Someone once told me that the most common word a child hears in the first 16 years of life is 'no'. ('No you cannot have an ice-cream.' 'No you cannot watch television.')

The word 'no' often becomes a subconscious automatic response to perceived future vexation and things we dislike. In this way 'no' safeguards our comfort zones. It is easier to say 'no' than 'yes'. 'No' is a constraining word. It disables and frustrates people. Many bosses are prone to saying 'no' rather than striving to find a 'yes' response. 'No' gives them power and enables them to become controllers.

Early in my career I made a conscious decision to say 'yes' to whatever challenges were presented to me at work. I cannot recall a single instance where I turned down a request for help. Even if I was overloaded with a backlog of work I would be willing to help out if asked. If my boss asked me for something I assumed it was a priority. So I would take on the extra work, reordering my own priorities accordingly.

In this way I gained a reputation as someone who was willing to help – rather than someone who was difficult and could always find reasons for saying 'no'. By saying 'yes' every time I learnt that I could stretch my capacity beyond what I had previously imagined. It exposed me to more learning opportunities as well as the chance to achieve much more through taking on big challenges. Even if my boss wanted to drop me in the deep end I would say 'yes', knowing that I would soon learn to swim.

There is a saying, 'Where there is a will there is a way.' This is equivalent to the power of saying 'yes'. It is the willing who make progress in their careers. It impresses bosses that you have a positive attitude and if you are asked to do something you will get on and do it, rather than pose difficulties. Positive people are imbued with the 'spirit of yes'. They take delight in saying 'yes' and are much admired in any organisation.

Equally important is how you say 'yes'. Never hesitate. Never plead, 'Can you give me some time to think about this?' 'Yes' should be a decisive and immediate response on your part. By seeking your help you should trust that the other person has correctly assumed you can provide it. Even when your boss invites you to take on a challenging assignment trust her judgement and agree on the spot. 'Yes, I'd love to take on that project!' You can think through the ramifications later and work out your plans accordingly.

The 'power of yes' teaches you to think in terms of opportunities whilst the 'power of no' leads you to see the world in terms of problems and difficulties.

However there are two important qualifiers to saying 'yes'. First, only say 'yes' to people you trust. When there is distrust there is a risk that the willing horse gets flogged (to use a cliché). But who would want to work in such an organisation?

Second, setting 'yes' as a default option does not mean agreeing with everyone's opinions and thus becoming an obsequious yes-man or lackey.

The 'yes' referred to in this chapter is 'yes to challenge' not 'yes to exploitation' or 'yes to submission'.

PRACTICAL TIPS

- Think five times before saying 'no' but only give a second's thought to saying 'yes'.
- Say 'yes' to opportunities.
- Avoid thinking in terms of problems and thus saying 'no'.
- Read the book *Yes Man* by Danny Wallace[1] and/or see the film of the same name starring Jim Carrey and Terence Stamp.

[1] *Yes Man*, Danny Wallace, Ebury Press, 2005

15

DON'T LET
PEOPLE DOWN

Honour these two well-known adages:

- 'Do as you say, and say as you do'
- 'Be true to your word'

When you really feel bad about letting someone down, even on a minor thing, you know you are en route to becoming a reliable person. Conversely if you blithely allow yourself to make excuses for non-delivery you are in danger of gaining a reputation as an unreliable person. It's your choice. Reliability is an essential characteristic of any person wanted for employment.

In any organisation there are two types of people. Those who are invariably reliable and those who are not. In certain professions, for example airline pilots, you expect total reliability. I would not fly on any airline where there was a hint of unreliable cockpit crews. I would expect the same of surgeons and house-builders.

House-builders? Many are not reliable. The last new 'high-quality' house I moved into in the UK had at least six defects. And by repute politicians are not reliable. Only a few deliver what they promise. They might conjure excuses, but in the end they are both unreliable and expedient.

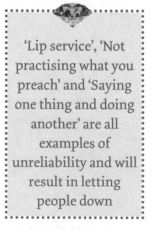

'Lip service', 'Not practising what you preach' and 'Saying one thing and doing another' are all examples of unreliability and will result in letting people down

Late deliveries, late trains and late responses are other examples of how unreliability infects our lives daily. Then there are the multitudes who fail to show up for work at the given hour. Unreliability is generated by people and causes others to become inefficient. In our highly pressurised world we risk an epidemic of unreliability.

The easiest thing is to cite external factors for the lack of reliability. A common example is when people blame traffic delays or 'being busy' for being late. Like politicians many people have a wide range of external excuses up their sleeves to explain why they did not honour their commitments. They always point to unforeseen circumstances. The best bosses will accept the excuse the first time, tolerate it the second time but take the unreliable person to task the third time.

With the exception of a dire emergency (which by definition is rare) there is no excuse for unreliability. The challenge for anyone who aims to be wanted by the best bosses is to create a 'reliability mindset' by which he or she will suffer immense shame on letting another person down.

In practical terms this means, for example:

(a) being punctual
(b) always delivering on schedule
(c) producing the agreed results on time every time
(d) having the information and documentation available when needed
(e) making commitments and keeping them (e.g. calling back at 2.00 pm as promised)
(f) being there when needed.

Reliability is an inviolate principle practised every day by those who want to get on in this world. They show up and never give up. They can be depended upon for essential support. They never let the side down and are essentially 100 per cent trustworthy. Actually they are a rare type of human being. To be wanted you need to be one of them.

PRACTICAL TIP

Prepare a mental checklist of the commitments you make every day and then be honest:

- Do you honour these commitments? If you do not make commitments you are essentially unreliable. Punctuality is but just one example. Keeping promises is another.

Career stimuli **4**

ACADEMY

- You, your work, your career and your life comprise an academy.
- You expel yourself from it at your peril.
- Do not blame your background or your school for a lack of learning.
- You are the teacher.
- Your world is a learning resource.
- Everything, everybody, everywhere is a learning resource.
- You create your own world through learning and application of the lessons.
- There is no progress without learning.
- You earn your future prosperity through learning.
- Only through learning will you be WANTED.

16

MEASURE UP

You cannot be successful in your work or your career without a measure of success

If you want to make progress or improve then measurement (qualitative or quantitative) should be a key element of your approach.

It is fashionable in modern management to have performance measures for everything. Often this results in having measures for the sake of measures with the consequence that there are too many, they are often meaningless and they bear little relationship to the outcomes desired by customers and shareholders alike.

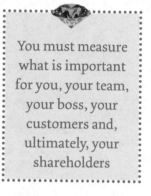

You must measure what is important for you, your team, your boss, your customers and, ultimately, your shareholders

However this is not to negate the importance of measures. How can a marathon runner improve her performance unless she has a measure of her time together with a target for improvement?

To make improvements it is essential that you have some measure of that improvement. If you are a sales person with a past performance showing you converted one in ten customer calls into sales worth 'x' then it makes sense to aim for two conversions per ten calls into sales worth '2x'.

A quantitative measure of success then becomes a valuable piece of data when being considered for a much-wanted job. Equally important are qualitative measures involving a degree of subjective judgement. You cannot measure the performance of a receptionist by how often she smiles or by the number of visitor commendations. Inevitably there will be a degree of subjective 'measuring up' determined by perceived attitudes, behaviours and overall approach to the work.

The key criteria for any measurement process for individuals are:

1 The measures must be simple (easy to understand and easy to measure).
2 The measures must be important and meaningful (by being linked to the desired outcome for the job).
3 The measures must be few in number (ideally between three and six).

When your measures meet these criteria they become memorable and can influence your daily behaviour in making improvements. An example of such behavioural improvements might relate to how you approach customers. Instead of just 'pushing product' at them you might improve by 'building relationships and understanding their needs'. You can measure your success through the resultant sales.

Ultimately you must not wait for or rely upon your organisation for the imposition of measures. If they are thrust upon you then accept them and work to them. However it is far better to initiate your own personal measures of success and work towards attaining these. In this way you can ensure the measures are important, meaningful and sufficiently substantial to impress those you wish to impress in the future.

PRACTICAL TIP

- Focus on one measure at a time and concentrate on this for the day or the week. Thus you might focus on an improved speed of response to customers. This is measurable, beneficial and substantial.

17

BE EXTRA-CURRICULAR

95 per cent of learning occurs outside the classroom and cannot be found in textbooks or in lectures given by the most highly esteemed professors

Create your own study plan to improve your current on-job performance and to further your career. Educate yourself with daily study modules.

Those who confine themselves to classroom learning, the study of textbooks and the simple pursuit of certification will limit their careers. In the university of life there is no limit to the curriculum. In pursuit of what you want (to become wanted) you need to set your own course of study. Your 'curriculum vitae' then literally becomes that – 'the course of your life' and the 'curricle' you have used to get there.

Most students will sit in their classrooms and obtain their grades. That much is easy and conventional. To excel in your career you need to take on extra studies, either formal or informal. This extends throughout your career. You should always be learning in a semi-formal and conscious way.

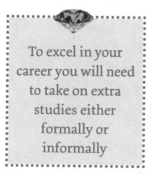

To excel in your career you will need to take on extra studies either formally or informally

It means studying books, reading professional journals, attending seminars by experts and soliciting the presence of wise people. It means mapping out your own path of study and pursuing it – perhaps to learn more about preventative maintenance (if you plan a career in building services or real estate management) or preventative health care (if you plan a career in occupational health).

If you are looking for a job as a bus driver you are more likely to be wanted if you have gone out of your way to learn about road safety, local areas of interest and customer service. The simple task of driving a bus is not enough. Excellent bus drivers are wanted because of their extra-curricular activities in their chosen profession.

No one can prescribe the course of your life, let alone the studies needed to achieve your ambition. When you emerge from school, college or university the one important thing you need to know is that you have so much more to learn. It is with post-graduation that the educational challenges really start. Those who rise to these challenges pursue extra-curricular activities at every stage of their life. For example, if they are pursuing a career in information technology they will have studied data protection even before the company puts them on the in-house course. They do not just rely on the company to train them, they train themselves. Successful people not only take advantage of the classroom training offered by their employers but search out and avail themselves of every other learning resource available. In this way they develop their expertise and become wanted.

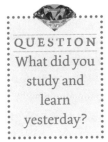

QUESTION
What did you study and learn yesterday?

PRACTICAL TIPS

- If you aim to be a team leader study psychology.
- If you aim to be a senior manager study history.
- If you aim to get on the board study anthropology.
- Spend at least two hours a week reading and studying learned journals.

18

BE IN THE
KNOW

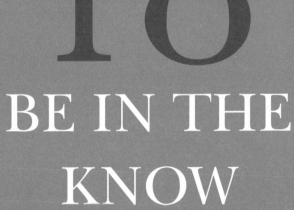

Be the first to find out and never the last to know

Every day get up to date with the news. Ensure you are 'in the know'. Read the latest news about the company in which you want to advance your career. Furthermore obtain the latest information about developments in your profession. Search the Internet to find out what's new. Build relationships with people who know what is happening to this company.

News is hot. Don't be left out in the cold by not knowing what is going on in the world around you. It is news that stimulates the world. Without it our daily lives would be that much more boring. You will also be seen as a bore if you never seem to be 'in the know'.

To promote yourself you need to be continually aware of what is happening both inside and outside your organisation. You also need to know what is happening in your profession. This requires keeping your ears to the ground and picking up all the signals of change that impact your team, your company, your expertise and your industry.

Keep your ears to the ground and pick up all the signals of change that will impact you and the team

Thus you will need to be in the know about oil prices, the value of the dollar and how these impact your place of work (or the place you want to work in). You will need to know what the competition is doing as well as how economic trends are affecting the market for your company's products and service.

Furthermore you will need to know about changes within your own organisation, for example relocation of premises, investments in new equipment as well as changes in the hierarchy. If the company appoints a new chief executive it is sensible to be in the know about his (or her) background. You might just bump into him in the lift!

The best way to keep in the know is to build relationships with others who are also in the know – then you will be the first to learn. Hot news normally travels much faster through relationship channels than through formal channels.

By being in the know you put yourself in an excellent position at interviews and any other 'career tests' to respond to questions such as, 'What are your feelings about the announcement made yesterday to relocate the production in our Midlands plant to Guangzhou in China?' Any declaration of ignorance will simply indicate your indifference about what is happening in the company. As such you will not be a 'wanted' person. For a start you had better know whereabouts in China the city of Guangzhou is (and even know how to pronounce the name).

QUESTION
Do you know about either the company's latest marketing campaign or any culture change programme?

Being in the know reveals a high degree of interest in the fortunes of the company and as such you are more likely to be 'wanted'.

Many professional institutes insist that members must allocate a given number of days annually to 'continued professional development' and thus keep in the know. It is important to comply with such requirements. However the people who are wanted the most go beyond such requirements. They are so passionate about their specialism that they regularly seek to update themselves on their subject. They scavenge for any news items, reports or learned papers that will help them enhance their own proficiencies in advising their clients or bosses. Google is an invaluable tool for this. They also look out for and study the latest tomes written by leading professionals as well as attend seminars and meetings presented by such experts.

Being in the know also relates to your customers, external or internal. In an increasingly competitive world most customers demand the best. They do not want a second-best physician or a third-rate computer technician. Thus most patients would prefer a doctor who is in the know about the latest drugs and their benefits and side effects.

If you are not in the know professionally you'll be seen as a third-rate hack

Furthermore when purchasing a new laptop most customers want a sales person who is in the know about comparative specifications of the two new competing models that came on the market yesterday.

PRACTICAL TIPS

Test yourself by trying to answer questions such as the following:

- 'Do you know how the organisation structure of the company has changed recently?'
- 'Do you know the history of the company – as well as its future plans?'
- 'Do you know in detail about the latest developments in your profession?'

19

LEARN SOMETHING INTERESTING EVERY DAY

With rare exceptions every single person in this world is interesting

Consider all your social encounters as a continuous and inexhaustible stream of learning opportunities. Take an interest in people and learn from them.

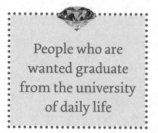

People who are wanted graduate from the university of daily life

With the exception of natural disasters all the problems in this world are caused by people. This includes wars, territorial conflicts, extremism, crime, accidents, divorces, family feuds, industrial disputes, strikes and personal grievances with rampaging bosses. People are not easy. They are complex both individually and collectively. Therefore it is almost a truism to assert the need for better understanding – of which there is still a dearth in this world. By comparison with people inanimate artefacts such as motor cars, aeroplanes and computers are simple to understand. After all it is people who designed them and put them together.

The pursuit of understanding people is best approached from a viewpoint that every single person in this world is of value and can offer fascinating insights and perspectives on conduct and attitude. This requires the elimination of prejudice and the adoption of humility. In conversation it requires a signal: 'I have so much to learn from you.' You might be the president, but even so you will have much to learn from the most lowly paid employee in the organisation.

The practical application of all this is to take an interest in the people you meet every day, whether known or unknown. As soon as you take an interest in other people you demonstrate that you value them as individuals. It shows that you respect (and are therefore non-judgemental of) their viewpoint of the world, their perception of the workplace and the workings of their hearts and minds. It reveals that you are keen to learn from them. The demonstration of such respect will earn their respect and will help the development of mutual understanding – the essence of harmony. As mentioned above, it is this essential understanding and harmony that is so deficient in our world.

Many individuals are far more interested in themselves than others. Such self-interest is endemic in many arenas and contributes to the conflicts we experience daily. As soon as you send a signal, directly or inadvertently, that 'I am more important than you – and therefore my interests should prevail' you risk a high degree of alienation.

Taking an interest in other people daily is easy. Rather than tell them about your journey to work Monday morning you should enquire about theirs. You should find out about their peregrinations and the trials and tribulations of their lives.

The more you learn about people, their cognitive processes and the desiderata of their waking hours the better the relationships you will have with most. You will be wanted for the simple reason that you understand.

The more you look for interesting things to learn (especially about people) the more you will find you become that interesting person everyone wants in their organisation.

PRACTICAL TIPS

- Every evening, on your return journey home challenge yourself to identify at least one interesting thing you learnt today (ideally about another person).

- When you attend an interview or an important meeting take an interest in the people present.

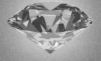

20

ORIGINATE
RESEARCH

Don't rely on others to give you the answers; research your own in your given area of expertise

Learn through original research (as well as that of others). Initiate research today on what it takes to be the best in your chosen profession and slowly build up a picture in your mind of how this differentiates from second-best (or worst). Then close the gap personally by aiming to be the best.

You can learn much by investigating other people's research and learning from it. However to be wanted by any organisation you need also to originate your own research.

Venture into the unknown and throw new light on some of the mysteries that excite your bosses

There is limited value in regurgitating published reports, data and conclusions to inform powerful professionals of what they already know. They might be reassured to learn that you know it too. However to impress important people, including a board of selectors, you need to venture into the unknown and throw new light on some of the mysteries that excite their interest. By using your own research and providing your own take on some of the key issues facing an organisation you will be able to convince the selectors of your potential contribution.

Initiating such research is not difficult. You can start by exploring the difference between the best and the second-best in your chosen field and garner fresh facts and evidence to illustrate the differentials. The chosen field might for example be motivation. Your research will indicate why one team is highly motivated and another less so. Another area might relate to customer service trends in the industry. Using your own support evidence you will provide your own take on what is happening together with your ideas for further improvement. Other fields might relate to safety, operational effectiveness or correlations between certain types of investment and long-term profitability.

You do not have to be a scientist working in a laboratory to undertake research, nor does your research require a formal programme of investigation and analysis. It is perhaps better to see it as an informal exercise in completing a jigsaw puzzle in which you search for missing pieces.

Research is motivational because it brings answers others do not have. We live in a world where so little is known and irrationality continues to override rationality. This is illustrated in the 2008 book *Flirting with Disaster (why accidents are rarely accidental)* by Marc Gerstein.[1] He cites for example cases of 'irrationality in financial decision-making' that led to disaster. The opportunity for organisational (and personal) improvement can often arise when 'in-house' research points to irrational decision making – leading to inefficient processes, unnecessary bureaucracy and disastrous decisions. There is so much scope for improvement as a result of research – and the people who are wanted are those who can initiate and undertake their own independent programmes for this.

QUESTION
What research are you currently undertaking to improve your current approach at work (or in your studies)?

---

[1] *Flirting with Disaster*, Marc Gerstein, Union Square, 2008

PRACTICAL TIPS

- Undertake customer research continually with a view to making improvements.
- Undertake research into the organisations you aspire to join.
- Undertake research into what motivates people in your organisation/community.

21

BECOME A 'CLASS ACT'

To become a class act you must experience 'live' other class acts

Set yourself a personal goal of devoting at least two days a year to experiencing class acts in your field. Then memorise and apply the lessons in order to become a class act yourself.

When you hear a top practitioner lecture something rubs off and a vital internal learning process takes place. The 'live' experience is well worth the investment. The same applies to the experience of attending a 'live' concert by a top orchestra (or rock group) in comparison to just listening to their recordings.

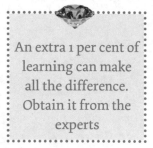

An extra 1 per cent of learning can make all the difference. Obtain it from the experts

The key to becoming a class act (and thus becoming much wanted in any organisation) is only to attend seminars presented by top-class people. This is why, in my opinion, so much in-house training is limited, especially in the soft skills of leadership, motivation and service. In-house trainers do not provide independent learning, biased as they must be by company doctrine. As such they will struggle to be the best. More often than not they just work to a training manual put together by someone else. You can hardly be a class act when the material is not your own. You need to be yourself.

Speakers who are class acts present their own original material. They offer a source not only of valuable experience and expertise, but of wisdom and inspiration. Their class acts will help you become a class act too. The benefits they offer will stay with you and come into use on many unforeseen occasions.

Over recent years I have twice attended talks by Alexander McCall Smith, who is not only a best-selling author but also a great speaker. Twice I walked away from his lectures a better person for the insights he presented and for the lessons he provided about writing and presentation. He had my mind racing after each occasion. Alexander McCall Smith is a class act.

I've encountered many others and have been fortunate in my time to attend presentations by Bill Gates (founder, Microsoft), Michael Dell (founder, Dell Computers), Jack Welch (ex-CEO, General Electric) and Sir Richard Branson (founder, Virgin Group). They were also inspirational and there were lessons from these class acts that have remained with me to this day. I could say the same of the musical conductor and leadership guru Benjamin Zander, whom I've gone out of my way to hear on five occasions, twice in Singapore and three times in London. These people have been key influences in my life and helped me, I hope, become a little more classier in the work I continue to do.

They have given me an extra one per cent of learning that has proved beneficial in many situations. Thus to become a class act you must be highly selective about the classes you attend in attempting to improve yourself. Most experts like to do a little teaching from time to time. So go and research their sessions and if necessary persuade your company to invest in your attendance. If it won't, make the investment yourself.

I came across a young man employed by one bank who was top of the bank's national league in terms of selling various banking products. In order to become a class act (selling banking products) part of his personal strategy was to invest his own money to attend sessions by world-renowned speakers such as Anthony Robbins. In other words, as his bank was not prepared to fund his learning he funded it himself. No wonder he became number one in his field and was wanted everywhere (by bosses and customers alike).

PRACTICAL TIPS

- Do not waste time attending boring seminars where all you do is look at your watch.
- Instead focus on what you need to learn and then seek out the experts in this field.
- Be prepared to travel the world at your own expense to experience 'class acts' and learn from their expertise. You will reap so many benefits from your investment.

22

LISTEN TO
WHAT PEOPLE
LISTEN TO

'Second-level' listening and influence provide you with a deeper understanding of where people are 'coming from' and what 'they are all about'

To be a successful listener you need to get beneath what people say. So go and study what they listen to and discover what influences them.

Dan Storper, founder and CEO of the record label Putumayo World Music, started playing world music in his original clothing and handicraft stores. He listened carefully to the music that made customers' ears prick up when shopping. This influenced him. So in 1993 he started a record label specialising in compilations of this type of music. Putumayo has been phenomenally successful. Nowadays Storper holds listening sessions for his employees before deciding which tracks to put on to a new CD. He thus allows his decision making to be influenced by his employees.

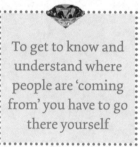

To get to know and understand where people are 'coming from' you have to go there yourself

It is not sufficient just to listen to what individuals say. To gain a deeper understanding you need to delve down to the next level and listen to what these individuals are listening to and discover what influences them. Thus if you know that your boss listens to Radio 4's *Today* programme every morning you will know what influences her thinking when she's talking about current affairs. So why not listen to *Today* to gain a deeper understanding of what makes your boss tick? This will surely enhance your relationship with her.

This second-level listening and exploration of influence will always serve you well. It doesn't mean that you have to like what you hear at this second level. Just because your boss is a fan of Wagner does not require you to become one too. Your boss won't encounter too many Wagner fans at work and when she discovers that you are at least interested and have heard some of Wagner's wonderful music this will improve your relationship no end.

As an 'internationalist' I am interested in the degree to which the USA influences this world. To that extent I followed the election and inauguration of President Barack Obama closely. I have listened to his speeches, watched him closely on television and tried to delve a little deeper into his psyche. For example Obama has been influenced substantially by President Abraham Lincoln. In my own voyage of 'second-level' discovery I have just finished reading an excellent biography of Lincoln by David Herbert Donald.[1] Next stop on this journey is Doris Kearns Goodwin's best-selling book *Team of Rivals*[2] about the political genius of Lincoln, a book that has influenced Obama greatly. By understanding Lincoln I will better understand Obama and in turn better understand the influence the USA currently has on the world.

The same principle of 'second-level' listening and influence applies to all people with whom you want to have a long-term (rather than superficial) relationship. If there are members of your team who are ardent Arsenal supporters then you had better understand what influences Arsène Wenger by listening to what he is saying on television, assuming he's still around by the time you read this. (For those of you who are not supporters of Arsenal Football Club I'm sorry – but I needed to pick one club to illustrate the point.)

[1] *Lincoln*, David Herbert Donald, Simon & Schuster, 1995

[2] *Team of Rivals*, Doris Kearns Goodwin, Simon & Schuster, 2005

The overall result of 'second-level' listening and influence is that you will be adjudged a person who has hidden depths – and for that you will be valued and much wanted.

In a television interview on 10 December 2008 Bill Clinton, ex-President of the USA, explained: 'I'm fascinated by different kinds of people in different circumstances. I was raised to be that way. I grew up in the pre-television age. I was 10 years old before my family got a television. My people were of modest circumstances, we never took vacations for example. So I was raised to take in as entertainment meeting different people and listening to their stories. That still influences me now in my current work.' He learnt to listen to what other people are listening to and thus discover what influenced them.

When you next go for an interview and your future boss asks, 'Do you have any questions for me?' I suggest the following response: 'I would be interested to learn who have been the key influences on your life.' If she then turns the question on you it is important you have your answer ready. Abraham Lincoln would be a good starting point!

PRACTICAL TIPS

- Set yourself a daily challenge of developing a deeper understanding of what people think and say.
- Do this by trying to listen to what they listen to and discover what influences them.
- Find out where their facts and opinions come from and then, if feasible, go to the original source and find out for yourself. (If a husband only listens to his wife then please disregard this advice.)
- Also review the key influences on your life, perhaps looking at your role models and those you aspire to be like.
- Overall, examine and study 'influence'.

Career stimuli (5)

HARD WORDS

- The *Concise Oxford English Dictionary* defines 240,000 words.
- The number of possible five-word sentences in English is 6.4 trillion.
- Effective communication is hard.
- Relationships exist through communication.
- Effective relationships exist through hard communication.
- Ineffective relationships arise from soft communication.
- Careers progress through communication.
- Determining what not to say is hard.
- Determining what to say is hard.
- Determining what words to use in saying anything is hard.
- Determining how to say them is hard.
- People who master the art of hard communication are WANTED.

23

CREATE
EVERYTHING
TWICE

All things are created twice. There's a mental or first creation and a physical or second creation to all things

Dr Stephen Covey

Before you perform on the day (however you define performance) first imagine yourself doing it.

To perform effectively you have to rehearse that performance, at least in your mind. This is closely aligned with the value of preparation, albeit here we are talking of mental preparation. One aspect of this is what Olympic athletes frequently call 'visualisation'. They will imagine themselves running the race and winning. They will imagine receiving the gold medal at the next Olympics.

The practice of visualisation, rehearsal and practice should apply to both long- and short-term goals and especially what is going to happen today and even in the next hour. How can you perform effectively (and thus fulfil your career ambition) unless you create a mental image of the steps you need to take daily?

When agendas become too full you risk rushing from one meeting to another without any prior thought about what to accomplish next. The day then becomes dominated by reactive responses as opposed to carefully thought-out proactive initiatives. Preparation and rehearsal are key factors in differentiating between those people who are wanted by organisations and those who are merely doers and reactors but hardly thinkers. It involves thinking through every activity you are about to undertake.

For example, before writing this chapter I rehearsed in my mind the key points I wanted to make and how the chapter would unfold. Inevitably when it came to the actual activity there was a degree of improvisation as new ideas sprang to mind – but overall I undertook a mental rehearsal of what I wanted to write.

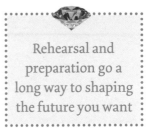

Rehearsal and preparation go a long way to shaping the future you want

The same should apply to any presentation you make to a senior team or statements you make at an interview relating to your next career move. When I was in mid-career I would often rehearse aloud at home presentations to the board or speak aloud in rehearsing my interview. Some of my family members thought I was barmy but such rehearsal enhanced the prospects of achieving what I wanted.

Whilst there is obviously merit in spontaneity and extemporisation such ad-libbing and impromptu responses are limited as forces for shaping the future. Rehearsal and preparation go a long way to ensuring progress in your career. You will come across as an assured person in command of your words. This will reassure decision makers that you give a lot of thought to what you say. You will be much wanted as a result.

PRACTICAL TIPS

- Keep in mind pictures of your overall goals, day by day and month by month, and then visualise the steps you will take to achieve each goal.
- Take a look at your schedule for next week, pick out the most important meeting and rehearse in your mind your approach to it.
- Remember the old saying, 'Practice makes perfect'. Practise everything in your mind first. This is 'mental rehearsal'.
- Always give yourself a few minutes before any major meeting or interview to reflect upon your previous 'rehearsal' and what you want to achieve.

24

TALK TO
STRANGERS

The easiest thing in the world is to talk with people you know. It's more difficult to talk with people you don't know

Every day challenge yourself to meet at least one person you've never met and initiate a businesslike relationship with her or him.

You will never be able to advance your career by sitting in a comfort zone – and one of the most comfortable things you can do is only chat to people you are comfortable with. Any observer of human nature will see this all the time – clusters of 'pals' who always sit together at meal breaks, groups of people from the same company who always gather round the same table at training courses. As a result cliques are formed and signals inadvertently sent out that strangers are not welcome. Communicating with strangers is hard work.

Successful people break through these barriers and are skilled at dealing with those they have never met before. It is a difficult skill to acquire but essential when applying for a job in another company where every person you meet, from the security guard through the receptionist and the HR expert

Successful people are skilled at dealing with people they have never met before

to the senior executive is a person you have never set eyes on before.

By developing the skill to talk to strangers you enhance your prospects of becoming the person every organisation wants. It shows that you have confidence and do not take the easy routine of confining your social interactions to your closest colleagues.

It demonstrates that you are well able to converse with customers and suppliers alike – and especially those difficult people with oscillating moods and eccentric behaviours. These are the strangers who are hard to deal with and who many prefer to shy away from. If you can talk sensibly with these people then you will be able to talk with anyone.

In business meetings with strangers it is best to enrobe the formal with the informal. This will humanise the relationship. For example, 'I'm so pleased you made it here with all the bad weather you've had down your way...' Your approach will obviously need to vary depending on the circumstance. This humanising of a new relationship is the hard part.

Another useful technique is to take an interest in whoever you encounter during your hours at work. By showing interest you demonstrate that you value the other person, even if you've never met him before.

Talking with strangers needs practice. Just chat to anyone who makes eye contact with you (and never look away when they do). You can start with innocuous questions such as, 'How was your journey this morning?' Many will ignore you but some will learn – about you. In practising this way you will gain confidence and be ready for that big moment when your strange new boss walks into your life. He will want you in his team for the simple reason that no other candidate asked him about his journey to work that morning.

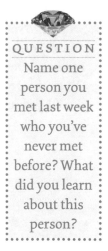

QUESTION
Name one person you met last week who you've never met before? What did you learn about this person?

On 20 January 2009 almost 2 million people crowded the National Mall and Pennsylvania Avenue in Washington to witness the inauguration ceremonies of President Obama. A frequent comment made by folks interviewed on television was, 'Everyone is so friendly and helpful, people are talking to each other.'

And that's how the world should be. And that's how your organisation should be. And that's how you should be. Remove the barriers protecting your comfort zone and get out into the world of business and talk to people!

PRACTICAL TIPS
- Initiate eye contact with people.
- Talk to the first stranger you encounter today who reciprocates your eye contact. (For example when you step inside the lift and see a face you don't recognise, just say, 'Good morning? How are you today?') The risk is you will be rebuffed, but the possibility is you will meet a fascinating person.
- Sit next to someone you don't know in the staff restaurant and initiate a conversation.
- Stroll into some unknown part of your company's premises and walk through the first open door you come across. Introduce yourself and ask: 'What goes on in here?'
- When you attend conferences always sit next to people you don't know and then initiate conversations with them.

25

EXPRESS
OPINIONS

When you have no opinions you will be written off as inconsequential

Challenge your own opinions. Prepare to be wrong. Only express opinions when you have mentally tested them inside and out. Convert opinions into suggestions. Never expect everyone to agree with you.

Opinions can be dangerous but they are essential. Opinions can get you into trouble but equally an absence of them can put you at a severe disadvantage, sidelining you amongst the forgotten people when key selections have to be made.

> Opinions have less to do with facts than your interpretation of the facts. It's what you believe the facts tell you

The soft option in any heated debate is not to express an opinion whilst the hardest thing is to risk an opinion that alienates everyone present. The aforementioned book by Marc Gerstein (*Flirting with Disaster*) highlights how some disasters occurred when people failed to venture a minority opinion for which they suspected they would be castigated. For them it was hard to speak up and challenge the opinion of bosses many grades up in the hierarchy.

The skill is not just in 'what you say' (this is difficult enough) but also in 'how you say it' (even harder). The people who are wanted in any organisation are those who have learnt to express opinions without alienating everyone around.

If you know your opinion is going to inflame the very person you seek to persuade then do not give it. Instead only express opinions to those prepared to listen to an alternative idea. Then you can have a fine discussion to flush out the best decision.

When disaster is imminent you have no option but to speak up and risk alienation by offering a minority opinion. Then your conscience will be clear.

Decision making is easy when there is certainty. No opinion is required. The facts are assured. Everyone agrees. Opinion comes into play when there is uncertainty. It can be argued that the better the debate the greater the probability of a good decision. When you do have doubts about the opinions of your colleagues there are two essential criteria to consider before coming to your own conclusions:

1 Keep your mind open to the possibility that the opinion of the person speaking is more valid than yours.
2 Never take it personally if someone expresses an opinion contrary to yours.

People who are really skilled at building relationships with others are those who listen carefully and work hard to elicit the opinions of others. They leave forming their own opinion until they have weighed up those of everyone else. When there are extremes of opinion they will then attempt to pull out the common denominators whilst discarding the points of disagreement. In this way opinions can be slowly changed and convergence achieved.

Expressing opinions requires the immense ability of knowing when to change your mind and when to continue arguing your case. The danger arises when others label you (and eventually reject you) as extremist for pursuing lost causes when it is clear the opinions of others hold better sway.

The people who are wanted by most well-run organisations are those who hold well-argued opinions about decisions to be made in the work situation. They will have an opinion on the proposed new uniform, on the content of the training programme about to be launched, on the refurbishment of the office, on changes to the roster, on how best to reduce costs or enhance sales revenue. They offer up their opinions as suggestions.

In a political democracy it is the opinion of the majority that counts, but no organisation I know, commercial or otherwise, acts as a democracy. It is the unelected bosses up and down the line who make decisions. The best ones are those who listen to and consider the opinions and suggestions of the team members they respect. You need to be one of them and express your opinions in the form of recommendations.

PRACTICAL TIPS

- Before you form any opinion get your facts in place and study them.
- Before you form an opinion solicit the opinions of any colleagues involved in the decision.
- Never personalise the opinion based on your own selfish interests .
- Demonstrate respect no matter how much you disagree with the other person's opinion.
- Try to convert your opinion into a suggestion.
- Always seek opportunities (especially at important meetings) to make suggestions based on your opinions.

26
TELL STORIES

Without stories there would be no human race. We'd all be animals

To tell great stories you need to listen to great story-tellers. For every story you tell listen to nine others.

Relationships are nourished with stories. They add a vital third dimension to communication and are as essential to human existence as food. Theories, facts, ideas and opinions are less assimilable, but better digested when steeped in a juicy tale. In the days of old, before the written word was invented, the way folk used to learn was through stories. The village elders would recount ancient myths and legends and these would in turn be passed down through the generations; whilst the facts would inevitably become embellished valuable lessons would be drawn.

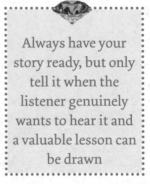

Always have your story ready, but only tell it when the listener genuinely wants to hear it and a valuable lesson can be drawn

The late Anita Roddick used to tell the story of how she opened the first Body Shop in Brighton in 1976 and in doing so learnt to challenge the status quo as well as learning the virtue of hard work. She also learnt the importance of passion and putting your soul into the business (hence the title of her 1991 book *Body and Soul*[1]). The lesson is there, in Anita Roddick's story.

Howard Schultz tells the tale of how, during a visit to Milan in 1983, he noticed the espresso bars on every street corner. 'The Italians,' he said, 'understood the personal relationship locals had with coffee. It was like an epiphany. Most American cafés

---

[1] *Body and Soul*, Anita Roddick, Ebury Press, 1991

had overlooked the central element – the social aspect.' It was through this visionary experience that Starbucks, as we know it today, was born. The lesson is there, in Howard Schultz's story (in his book *Pour Your Heart Into It*[2]).

Everyone has a story to tell, especially of how they arrived at where they are now. The skill of the story-teller is not just in the story but in how it is told and in the lessons a listener draws from it. A story that is all about 'me' (the story-teller) will alienate a listener, whilst a story which helps 'you' (the listener) is invaluable. As mentioned above, people learn through stories. Furthermore great stories are motivational as well as inspirational. The story of the rise of Abraham Lincoln, from dire poverty and minimal education to become president of the USA is an inspiration. Similarly with Barack Obama and his journey from a broken home to become the most powerful man in the world.

Stories form the cornerstones in building relationships. This is particularly important when going for a new job. At those critical moments during a crucial meeting or interview it is useless just stating facts. These are unlikely to be registered in the minds of people present. The facts only come alive when they are woven into a fine short story from which a lesson can be drawn. The key adjective here is 'short'. Sometimes two sentences are short enough. For example: 'Last year our star performer was Patricia, who sold an extra 200 units due to her rigour in following up with customers. We incorporated her self-taught techniques into our sales training programmes and now, year to date, we are 15 per cent ahead of target.' The lesson is in the story. The people who are wanted are those who can tell good stories.

---

[2] *Pour Your Heart Into It*, Howard Schultz, Hyperion, 1997

The purpose of stories is to bring the essential facts to life by stimulating the interest of the listener. Your career history will be full of facts but you need to bring these alive with some entertaining stories.

I was born during the Second World War. There was food rationing. After the end of the war sweets 'came off' rationing and every Saturday my grandmother would bring my brother and me a chocolate bar. This was one of the high points of our week and it stimulated an ambition that one day I would work in a chocolate factory. When I was 26 I joined the company Mars Ltd and began making chocolate bars. I fulfilled my ambition. That's my story.

As youngsters we had no television. I would occasionally daydream and stare at my parents' best Wedgwood china displayed in the cupboard in our dining room. On the blue dinner plates were scenes of willow trees, pagodas and quaint bridges with people in Chinese garb strolling over them. It portrayed a world I did not know and sparked a dream that one day I would travel to faraway places including China. I've now visited over 60 countries in my life and have been to China five times in the last two years. My dream came true. That's my story. (During my lectures in China my translators often struggle with the different meanings of the word 'China': the country and the best china you dine from.)

When you go for that interview tell the story of how your dreams and ambitions connect to the job you are applying for and which you very much want.

PRACTICAL TIPS

- Always wrap into a short story any important point you wish to communicate. This sets it in context.
- Your story should always be aimed at helping a listener benefit from a lesson, rather than impress the listener about your prowess.
- It is quite acceptable to embellish your story as long as its kernel is centred on the facts.

27

SCRIBBLE
NOTES

When on the move a scrap of notepaper is far more effective than a laptop

It's a great challenge to capture the words you want to recall. Use any old paper for this purpose.

During a keynote talk (at the Institute of Director's Annual Conference at the Royal Albert Hall, London, on 27 April 1993) Sir Richard Branson, founder of the Virgin Group, stressed the importance of carrying a notebook. Like many other inspirational leaders he is a keen listener and prepared to learn from his customers and

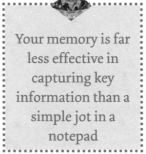

Your memory is far less effective in capturing key information than a simple jot in a notepad

employees alike. He argued that unless you jot something important down you risk losing the valuable information forever.

Without pen and notepaper handy there is a risk that a key message goes in one ear and out the other. The valuable things that people say then get lost and are not acted upon, let alone kept for future reference.

In my opinion a scrap of paper (or notepad) is far more effective than any portable laptop. It is so easy to use. You don't need to boot it up before capturing the word of the moment! You can use pen and paper on a train, a plane or even when waiting to pay at the checkout. You can readily scribble down the name of the front-liner who gives you excellent service and then subsequently drop an email to her boss. You can jot down a telephone number on a promotional poster for future follow-up. You can list people to contact over the next few days or you can note down titles of books recommended to you. If you hear a memorable quote a blank sheet of paper is invaluable for capturing it. You can even write down any important ideas you have!

The discipline of note taking will enhance the information available to you in improving your performance on the job as well as developing your career. You can use your laptop later to transcribe the notes and get them into actionable order.

I am always surprised by the large number of people who do not practise note taking. I am currently staying in a hotel where the service is a little lacking. I ask to see the duty manager. He comes along and I give him some feedback that I hope he will find helpful. But then I observe that he does not take notes of what I am saying. He just nods, smiles, says 'Yes' and 'Thank you for letting me know' and disappears.

The very first time I attended a presentation by Tom Peters (the co-author of the 1982 business classic *In Search of Excellence*[1] and one of the world's leading business speakers) I returned home with 20 pages of notes. I typed them up afterwards and because of these notes I can still refer to the key lessons 20 years later. We should not rely on memory alone.

Memory is fallible unless you are a genius such as Shakuntala Devi, known as the human computer and who calls herself India's 'Maths ambassador'. She has such a phenomenal memory that she can undertake amazingly large mathematical calculations in her head. Most of us are not like her, indeed we are quite forgetful. Yesterday I was introduced to a new neighbour's wife. Instantly I forgot her name. How dreadful! I used to know the daughter of the late entertainer known as the 'memory man', whose speciality was memorising key sports results going back

---

[1] *In Search of Excellence*, Thomas J. Peters and Robert H. Waterman Jnr, Harper & Row, 1982

decades. But for weeks I could not recall his name. (Actually it was Lesley Welch.) Aid your memory with a scrap of notepaper and a pen.

PRACTICAL TIPS

- Colour up your life by having seven different pocket-size notebooks, with seven different colours for each day of the week.
- Get into the habit of carrying a notepad and pen with you all the time. You never know when you are going to need it. (I find the notepads provided in most hotel rooms invaluable for this purpose.)
- Devote half an hour at the end of every week (or at the end of the day) to transcribing key notes into the 'notes file' on your computer. Keep these notes files for ever.
- Refer to your notes periodically so that you can reinforce the key lessons.

28

KISS

Keep it short and simple

The toughest words are those you should cut out.

It is easy to speak or write at length without realising a shorter statement would suffice. It was Blaise Pascal, the French philosopher who in 1656 wrote: 'I am sorry this letter is so long but I did not have time to make it shorter.' (This quotation is often attributed to George Bernard Shaw.)

However too much hard pruning of words will result in a summary that has little impact whilst no pruning will lead to verbosity and equal lack of impact. Striking a balance requires immense skill and places great demands on an effective communicator. Verbiage is like

Take time to edit ~~everything you plan to say or write~~ your communications

bindweed and difficult to eradicate. Concision therefore needs to be practised by way of a rigorous review of any statement. *You should be ruthless in excising words, phrases, sentences or paragraphs that are either repetitive or redundant.* Or perhaps I should write: *'Be ruthless in excising words that are redundant'*!

Here is an example of redundant adverbs and adjectives: *'Actually as far as your own job is concerned I really would not do this.'* The words *'actually'*, *'own'* and *'really'* are unnecessary. It is better to say: *'As far as your job is concerned I would not do this.'*

There are two additional benefits of keeping your communication short. First, it simplifies what you have to say and, second, it is easier to remember. Most people's recall is limited. They would rather receive short and simple statements that you can elaborate upon later should they so desire.

~~People who are wanted in any organisation are those that can speak and write in a simple and concise way.~~ People who are wanted can communicate succinctly.

~~To practise what I have been preaching I am going to end this chapter here~~...

To practise what I preach this chapter ends here...

29

FINE-TUNE
YOUR VOICE

Develop a voice that turns people on

Every day try to 'listen in' to the sound of your own voice. You will know when your voice is perfectly tuned – people will pay attention to you. Words come easy. What is difficult is how you say them.

Listen carefully when people are around. You will hear squeaky voices, inaudible voices, loud voices and when in meetings, monotonously boring voices. Others have euphonious voices that are a joy to listen to. Be one of them. Learn to project your voice in a way that compels people to listen to you without alienating them with a dominant shouting tone. For two great examples go to YouTube and listen to the late actor Richard Burton being interviewed by Sir Michael Parkinson. You will hear two compelling and mellifluous voices.

Be a person whose voice is a joy to listen to

The voice is multi-faceted, and with the exception of opera singers, stage actors and public speakers much ignored as an instrument for connecting with people. Most of us rely on our 'default' voice without exploring ways of developing it to express ourselves. This 'default' voice is a product of our upbringing and most times we are unaware of how it sounds and the impact it has on others. Tone, pace, clarity, intensity and intent as well as vocabulary and idiom are vital factors in determining the communicative impact of our voice. In other words to 'tune in' to people we have to fine-tune our voices.

The variety of options for fine-tuning is vast. The skill of persuasion is not just a matter of the words we select but also of the way the words are voiced. Articulation is one of the arts needed for a successful career and requires the exercise of vocal nuance for maximum impact.

This art of articulation thus evolves from our choice of words as well as our choice of tone, pace, clarity, intensity, intent and statement length. When these are perfectly combined what we say will appeal to the listener. Here are some hypothetical examples.

FINE-TUNING YOUR VOICE

FACTORS	Inappropriate choice (example)	Appropriate choice (example)
CHOICE OF WORDS	'Allo, I've gotta interview at 9 with the boss of HR.'	'Good morning! [pause] My name is Jo Wild and I'm here for a 9.00 am appointment with Mrs Hill.'
TONE	Cold/uncertain/ disrespectful/tiresome	Warm/respectful/ positive/cheerful
PACE	Too fast	Variably paced
CLARITY	Muffled, slurring of words, poor choice of words	Clear articulation, good choice of words
INTENSITY	Too harsh and uncouth	Genuine and confident
INTENT	Matter of fact	Puts the listener at ease and makes her happy

Modulation of the voice requires energy and a high degree of consciousness of how we sound to another. In working our voice we need to be sensitive to the effect our words have on others. We need to be asking ourselves, 'Have I really caught the attention of this person? Is she listening or just hearing?' Emotional tone is significant here. The amount of feeling pumped into any one word or short phrase will register with the listener who will interpret it as a sign of a candidate's sincerity or disinterest accordingly.

In conclusion it is worth quoting from the book *The Inner Voice*[1] by the opera singer Renée Fleming: 'It all comes down to two little pieces of cartilage in my throat. Those vocal cords – delicate, mysterious, slightly unpredictable – have taken me to unimaginable places.'

PRACTICAL TIPS

- Listen carefully to other people's voices and gauge the impact these have on you, then choose to emulate the one that has maximum impact.
- Try to record your own voice and listen carefully to how it sounds. Ask yourself: 'Is this the way I really want to sound?' If not, practise developing your voice to your sound.

[1] *The Inner Voice*, Renée Fleming, Virgin Books, 2005

30

TO BE GOOD LOOK FOR THE GOOD

Give credit where it is due and people will become indebted to you

Look for the positives in everyone you encounter on a daily basis, and then find ways of reflecting these back to them. Praising is the name of the game.

What you look for you often find. If you look for problems then you will find them around every corner. There is one person I know who defines life in terms of problems. Every day brings him a new set of problems. It's a mindset issue – whether you look for the good or bad in life. There's plenty of both around.

It's easy to locate the bad and to criticise. Our daily papers are replete with bad news. I was reading a tabloid today and only one of the ten headline stories was positive (and that related to a British sporting success). It does seem that we relish news about others' problems, whether it be the downfall of a politician or the demise of a celebrity as a result of scandalous behaviour.

Looking for the good in your colleagues will help you become a good colleague

Yet in our own daily lives we welcome good news when it is directed to us personally. We need to reciprocate this. Our challenge is to be continually impressed by our colleagues, bosses, future bosses – and the people we encounter daily. The opportunities to identify such positives are ubiquitous.

To rise to this challenge means abstaining from all criticism except when it is welcomed as a means of helping a colleague improve. Criticism that seeks to hurt (by making an individual feel bad) is not the tool of the person who wants to beome wanted in any organisation.

It is far better to seek out the behaviours, attributes and successes (no matter how minor) of which you approve and then praise these with a simple compliment. Most of us welcome approval, irrespective of who it comes from. Such approval enhances our sense of self-worth. So it is great to know that our boss has observed us come in early to meet an urgent noon-time deadline – and has expressed her approval accordingly. It is great to know that we are admired for our hard work, integrity and high standards. This can prove highly motivational.

Even visiting a new company (for example for an interview) provides opportunities to look for the good and reflect it back. On walking in to meet your prospective new boss you might say: 'If you don't mind me saying, I do like the view from your office', or 'By the way I was impressed by your secretary. She is so charming, efficient and helpful. She really put me at my ease.'

PRACTICAL TIPS

- Look for the good and reflect it back approvingly.
- Set yourself a challenge of complimenting or praising at least one person every day.
- Ensure the compliment is both genuine and sincere. False compliments will quickly erode your reputation.

31

WEAVE NETWORKS

The larger the network you develop the greater the probability of progress in your career

Remember that the network is a two-way process. You are there to help people on the network as much as they are there to help you.

There is an old adage, 'Business is built on relationships'. When there is no personal relationship there is no bond, no loyalty and little to stop a customer or employee defecting in favour of a better deal. For example, I used to have a relationship with my bank. This was conducted through the branch

A personal network is an informal mutual support system

manager and his immediate team, whom I knew well. That relationship was destroyed years ago with the advent of remote banking, call centres in distant parts and the frustrating struggle to communicate effectively with an understanding human being. In destroying the relationship I had with the local branch the bank destroyed my loyalty.

Relationships are personal and they facilitate good business and good employment. Little progress can be made in a career or in any job of work without good relationships. It means building a network of contacts. For each contact there should be a mutually beneficial relationship. You are more likely to get your computer fixed if you have an excellent relationship with the computer expert. Conversely you are more likely to put yourself out for someone you know personally than for a faceless 'name' extracted from a database.

Once you've met a person face to face you are also more likely to remember him or her. Any interaction then becomes personalised. We human beings are social animals and few of us want to rely solely on the computer screen for our interactions with others. Internet products such as 'Facebook' and 'Friendster' will definitely appeal to many but they can never offer the reality of genuine acquaintance, friendship and personal contact.

Individuals described as 'loners' might well stick to their technology and impersonal equipment for life's satisfactions, but those who make progress in their organisations and their industries are those who develop an extensive network of contacts who they rely on for help and guidance in time of need as well as reciprocating as required.

The provision of references (or the use of referees) is just one example of the value of networks. Few people get a new job without the new boss checking out the successful candidate by way of reference. When you have a wide network of contacts it will never prove difficult to find two or three people who can vouch for your prowess in a given field of endeavour. Another example is when you need advice on a particular topic – you will know exactly who to turn to in your network to help you.

Similarly the network can be used for opening doors and meeting influential people who would otherwise deny you the time of day.

The advantage of an extensive network is that it can help you get the job you want. You will become wanted because it will be obvious that you know a lot of people in the industry or profession. Your contact list will prove an invaluable asset.

PRACTICAL TIPS

- Seize every opportunity to meet new people both outside your company and within it.
- Collect their business cards and always follow up to reinforce the new relationship.

Career stimuli **6**

THE GAME

- The game is cricket.
- The game is chess.
- The game is competitive.
- The game is your career.
- The game has rules.
- The game has unofficial rules.
- At times you make up your own rules.
- People who keep to the official rules are bureaucrats.
- People who know when to break the rules are wanted.
- It is the people at the top of their game who are WANTED.

32

JUMP SHIP

Don't become a coastal mariner. Jump ship and sail over the horizon

Keep moving, that's the name of the game. Once every four years take a good look at what is on the high sea of opportunity and start pitching for exciting new jobs elsewhere.

Shinji Hattori is not only president and CEO of Seiko Watch Corporation but a great-grand-son of Kintarõ Hattori, who founded the company in 1881. Many employees spend the whole of their working lives with Seiko. The company bases its success on continued innovation and refinement of technology and this is fostered amongst its many loyal employees, technical experts and managers.

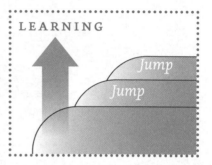

Seiko is the exception that proves the rule.

Nowadays the success of any family business will depend on bringing in professional managers and experts from outside. For example Cadbury is one of the UK's greatest companies, founded as a family business in 1824 by John Cadbury. Yet today you will not find one single member of the Cadbury family on the board, let alone on the chief executive's committee. Even so the original ethos of the company, 'Doing good is good for business' remains part of its culture. Furthermore, when you study the profiles of the top 20 executives at Cadbury you only find one (at the time of writing) who started his career with Cadbury. All the other members of the senior team have had experience elsewhere.

In my own case, I had worked with four other companies before being appointed to the board of an airline. There is a high risk that if you stay with the same company all your career your learning curve flattens out (see diagram opposite) even if the company moves you around. To enhance your value and become wanted it is thus essential that you 'jump ship' every few years to gain new experience and learning. You will benefit from a new culture, different ways of working, and from joining a team of people you hardly know.

A further risk of staying with the same company is of complacency and arrogance. Inevitably you will limit your horizons and be unable to see what others who have been there (over the horizon) see.

Personally I became restless when stuck in the same job for years. I stayed with one company for six years and that was much too long. After the initial learning curve of perhaps three or four years I became bored with a repetition of the same old problems. I needed a completely new challenge and something fresh to stimulate my intellectual and emotional appetite.

To become wanted in your career you have to soak up and apply experiences, knowledge and skills that will be of value to other organisations. You limit the probability of this happening by sitting in the same chair for years and staring at the same computer screen, let alone attending the same old committees every week.

PRACTICAL TIP

- Ask yourself every weekend, 'What am I learning in my current job? What great experiences am I getting?' When you draw a blank it is time to move on and explore new horizons.

33

BE VISIBLE

You need to be seen in the right places at the right time

Get outside the circle of the people you encounter every day and ensure you leave your 'mark' with influential people.

Some people stand out in a crowd. You need to be one of them. You need to catch the eye of the people who count. This has little to do with the way you dress and more to do with your overall demeanour and expressiveness.

If you are not visible in the organisation you'll be left in the dark

Most senior people are wise enough to know that from time to time they have to descend into the depths of the organisation to meet employees and junior managers many ranks below them. This happens for example at retirement events, conferences and annual gatherings as well as at Christmas parties. It also happens during 'walkabouts', charity functions and sports contests. As a front-liner, team leader or middle manager you need to be there. You need to be visible.

As a board director I worked for a company with over 7,000 employees. It was impossible for me to know all of them. On average, once a week I would dedicate a whole evening, as representative of the board, to attend a function for employees, chat to them and give an impromptu speech. Invariably I would enter a large room with hundreds of people sipping drinks and chatting away. I would know none of them. They were all strangers to me – although most of them would recognise me from photos in the company newspaper. I could hardly stand in a corner gazing into my drink. My job was to initiate conversations, take an interest in whoever I was talking with – and listen to what they had to say.

If nobody approached me I would ask myself, 'Who should I talk to?' My choice was always the same. I would talk to anybody who caught my eye and sent me body language signals that they would welcome a chat. You need to be that person whenever a senior person is in your vicinity. It puts them at ease and it makes them feel they are doing what all good senior people do – chat from time to time with front-liners. You will need to ensure you leave your 'mark' (by saying something important) and also ensure they recall your name and department.

By becoming visible you will be entered on the mental database of influential people at the top. When a challenging opportunity arises and senior people are seeking help from the ranks you will be one of the first they think of. You will have been earmarked as 'rising talent'.

By becoming visible and engaging with decision makers you develop confidence that you can chat to anyone. You should never become an employee who shies away from senior people, fearful you may say the wrong thing and make a fool of yourself.

Visibility also extends to consultative meetings at work. Should a senior executive be chairing a session then make sure you catch his or her eye. Make sure you ask a sensible question or say something helpful. It is all about being seen and then heard. If you are never seen there is little chance you will be considered.

PRACTICAL TIP

- Try to attend as many company functions as possible and challenge yourself to chat with at least one of the senior executives present. If there are top people visiting from other companies try to leave your mark with them too... you never know!

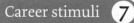

Career stimuli 7

PSYCHE

- It is estimated that the brain has up to 100 billion nerve cells.
- The eye sends 10 million bits of data to the brain every second.
- During our waking hours we are unconscious most of the time.
- You are a complex individual.
- You don't see yourself the way others see you.
- You are not what you think you are.
- How you make up your mind will be influenced by the make-up of your heart.
- Your career is a product of your psyche.
- Those who have a good informal understanding of psychology are those who will be WANTED.

34

BE QUIETLY CONFIDENT

It is not enough for you to be confident

Being quietly confident requires that you lack a little confidence and therefore are always seeking to develop it further. Never be 100 per cent sure that you are always right. No matter how confident you are you could always be wrong.

For some people confidence can be a liability whilst for others it is an asset. To achieve any degree of trust and respect it is important that people feel confident about your abilities. Confidence then becomes an asset. When you are overconfident people lose confidence in you.

Whatever your knowledge and experience the confidence you display has to be tempered by the response of your intended audience, whether it is your future boss in a one-to-one interview or a gathering of 200 frontliners. This means being quietly confident as you listen and carefully take in what people say. In this way you can fine-tune your communication and convince people that you know what you are talking about. You will also show that you are responsive to their needs.

People will lose confidence in you if you are overconfident

Today before writing this I watched a political panel debate on television. One panellist was so confident about her opinions (about which candidate and which policies were best) that she seemed to alienate the audience. She certainly alienated me. She was overconfident and too loud. She spoke so forcefully that she appeared intolerant of dissent. In fact when another panellist dared challenge her she simply ridiculed him, saying he did not know what he was talking about. It is possible he did not, but she seemed incapable of listening to let alone understanding a contrary viewpoint. I sensed she had convinced herself she was right and her mission was to convince others of this too. She lost the argument and the debate vote went to the other side.

People who are quietly confident (and thus humble) are so much more impressive than those overconfident people who appear arrogant and often harangue their hearers. These loudmouths (or blowhards) think they know so much they spend their whole life telling others the answers. There is an ancient Chinese adage that 'A wise man knows nothing whilst a fool knows everything'.

To be quietly confident you need to hold back that urge to impress others with your mastery. Even at important interviews first listen carefully and then ensure that what you say gives confidence. In addition to knowing your subject well it means speaking

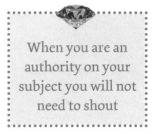

When you are an authority on your subject you will not need to shout

with an assured and authoritative voice. When your listeners gain confidence in you not only will they start nodding discreetly in agreement but their eyes will become wider and more focused on yours. You will be opening their eyes as they begin to realise that the expertise you have to offer meets their requirements.

PRACTICAL TIP

- Hold up a metaphorical mirror to yourself and ask, 'How do I come across at meetings?' If you are really brave enough ask your boss or colleagues, 'Do I come across as overconfident, underconfident or quietly confident in the right sort of way?'

35

VOLUNTEER

Volunteering is the essential practice of giving more than you are contracted for

Volunteering demonstrates that you have a positive, proactive attitude towards you work. It will not go unnoticed. Be a mindful volunteer.

Always be the one to raise your hand when your boss asks for a volunteer. Too often there will be an uneasy silence and people will mumble to themselves, 'I'm too busy' or 'I've got too much on my plate already'.

It doesn't matter. No matter what is on your plate volunteer for more. In theory there is a limit to what you can do during sensible hours of hard work but in practice there is always scope for more.

It is the volunteers who get noticed. It is the volunteers who are wanted in any organisation

It is the volunteers who get noticed, who get extra points during those crucial moments of summing up when top executives decide who should get the job. Volunteering is also fun. It brings new experiences and challenges together with a break from the daily grind. Volunteering refreshes the mind and provides a stimulus to explore new territory.

Furthermore do not just volunteer for the 'juicy jobs' (the two-week project in Cape Town) but also for those jobs nobody else wants to touch (addressing the congestion problem in the company car park). I recall attending my first senior executive meeting when the chief executive commented, 'We really do need someone to sort out the car parking problem – it's been festering for such a long time.' Everyone looked at me – the new boy. I volunteered. Another colleague later informed me I had taken on a poisoned chalice – nobody had been able to sort out the car parking problem in five years. It was sorted.

Volunteering can relate to any type of job and to any activity, whether it is volunteering to work over the weekend to clear up a major backlog of work or to take a six-month secondment 'up North' to resuscitate an ailing branch operation.

In terms of motivation seeking volunteers is far more effective than imposing additional tasks on unwilling employees. The use of volunteers becomes a helpful selection tool as it identifies those who are more motivated than others, more hard working, more imaginative and more prepared to stretch themselves.

The corollary is that if you volunteer you must do it. There are people who volunteer and then neglect the very task they have taken on board. This happens in organisations where people are rarely called to account and lame excuses are accepted at face value. To be an effective volunteer you must be serious about the new project in addition to any ongoing work you are still responsible for.

PRACTICAL TIP

- Do not hesitate when your boss seeks a volunteer for an important project. Be the first to raise your hand – irrespective of your current workload. You will manage and everyone will benefit.

36

SET YOURSELF
BOUNDARIES

There are personal boundaries you should never cross

Your everyday behaviour is guided by the boundaries you have in your mind.

To keep on the right side of organisation acceptability and avoid transgression you need to be clear about your own personal boundaries of performance, conduct and attitude. Without clear boundaries you will wander all over the place and be classified as a deviant.

Let's take performance for example. You need to have a clear boundary in your mind that differentiates unacceptable from acceptable performance on your part (see diagram).

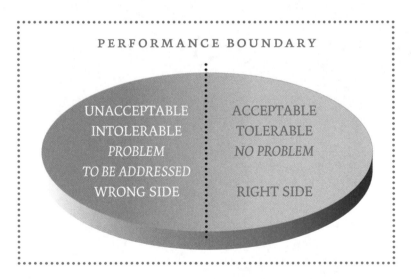

PERFORMANCE BOUNDARY

UNACCEPTABLE	ACCEPTABLE
INTOLERABLE	TOLERABLE
PROBLEM	*NO PROBLEM*
TO BE ADDRESSED	
WRONG SIDE	RIGHT SIDE

You could set the same personal boundaries for acceptable/unacceptable conduct and attitudes. It requires personal discipline to ensure you do not err on the wrong side of all these boundaries.

Many decades ago, in my first job ever, there was an older Cockney woman working alongside me in the laboratory. She was very friendly but always teasing me. To get my own back I once crept up on her and tapped her on the bottom. She turned quickly and with a disapproving smile said, 'Don't ever do that again!' It was a valuable lesson. I had crossed a boundary on to the wrong side.

It is no good relying on your boss to set the boundary of performance. You have to work it out for yourself. You will need a similar line in your mind relating to conduct and attitude. This will be based on your own personal ethic and will determine (for example):

- whether or not you swear, as many do;
- whether or not you are always on time or are late, as many are;
- whether or not you talk behind people's backs, as many do;
- whether or not you accept low-quality work, as many do;
- whether or not you tolerate humour based on prejudice (e.g. making fun of a minority group).

People who are fuzzy about their boundaries (of performance, conduct and attitude) or have none in their mind readily lose respect and are difficult to deal with. Few people will know where they stand with them. The personal boundaries you set create that understanding. They give you strength and enhance the respect others will have for you. They will not 'mess' with you because they know you will not tolerate let alone display such transgression. Equally you will not 'mess' with them when you know their boundaries.

In one transport company I worked for (as a consultant) it seemed that every other front-liner used the 'f' word in every other sentence. The easier decision would have been to cross the boundary into obscenity and use the word myself (and thus become 'one of the boys'). The more difficult decision was whether or not to confront such behaviour and try to eradicate it. I didn't. I tolerated it.

Other examples relate to 'whistle blowing' and reporting colleagues who go beyond the boundaries of acceptable behaviour. Ultimately the line between acceptable/unacceptable performance, conduct and attitude is one that only you can provide. It is up to you to generate these boundaries and then never cross them.

Similarly, whilst keeping to your own boundaries it is essential to determine and respect the boundaries set by others.

PRACTICAL TIP

- Review your boundaries of performance, conduct and attitude when it comes to work. If you struggle with this then you need to retreat for a few days and go through a process of re-establishing these boundary lines.

37

NEVER
COMPLAIN

People who always complain burn themselves

Complaining can become a habitual state of mind. If you have acquired this then it is imperative to change states. Develop the art of positive suggestion by trying to help the person you would previously have complained about.

An instinctive reaction is to complain about what is wrong. With all the imperfections evident in companies it is easy to highlight deficiencies and weaknesses, especially of people not in the room. There is a false assumption that by complaining you impress others with the incisiveness of your perceptions and the excellence of your

Professionals don't complain, instead they make constructive suggestions

opinions. Whilst others keep quiet or remain tolerant you hope to be seen as the courageous one who speaks out against malpractice. You develop expertise in pointing out the inadequacies of others, about their lack of action or the mistakes made when the wrong action is taken. You become part of the fault-finding vocal minority.

Unfortunately it is much easier to see a negative than a positive. Our genetic make-up has been developed to warn us of threats and potential pain. So we are pretty good at identifying negatives. The process of complaining is one defence mechanism we use frequently for this purpose. It averts the focus from our own weaknesses and attempts to concentrate attention on the weaknesses of others.

Sadly most complaints are counter-productive. If there is one complaint about people who regularly complain it is that they alienate people with their persistent moans and groans. The skill is to convert the negative, upon which the complaint is based, into a positive. This can be done using the 'art of suggestion'. This requires integrity. Rather than complain about a person behind their back, as many do, it is far better to go and see this person and humbly make a suggestion for change and improvement.

When it comes to interview time then you should apply a strict rule not to complain about your current boss or the company you work for, no matter how tempting this is to justify your application. Whilst most companies are full of faults (as stated above) recruiters and people in power detest fault finders. The people they want are solution providers rather than problem staters. They want positive people who are skilled and experienced in seizing opportunities for the good of all, rather than experts in aggravation.

The danger of becoming a veteran complainer is that it will drag you down personally and burn away your spirit. There is enough wrong with this world for you to complain forever. The people who are wanted are those who never complain.

This is not to advocate a process of denial whereby we refuse to acknowledge and accept our organisation's imperfections. The fact is they do exist. The challenge is not to waste energy complaining about them but to focus our energies on the deficiencies we can do something about. In this way we eliminate negatives and make positive improvements. When you can demonstrate this you will be much wanted.

PRACTICAL TIPS

- Bite your tongue and think twice before making any complaint, formal or informal.
- Only use complaining as a safety valve with people you are very close to and can trust completely. (Sometimes it is good to get things off your chest – but there is no need to tell everyone.)
- A much more pertinent question to ask is, 'Do people ever complain about me?' You need to know the answer and take action accordingly.
- If you feel like complaining convert it into a positive suggestion.

Career stimuli 8

EXTREMES

- Those who work in comfort zones are at extreme risk.
- By pursuing extremes outside your comfort zone you minimise risk.
- Progress can only be made by the pursuit of extremes.
- Successful people go to extremes to achieve what they want.
- 110 per cent is an extreme when you are expected to give 100 per cent.
- Extremes are not defined by existing boundaries but reached by going beyond them.
- Extremes are a product of passion, not of reason.
- Only work for an organisation that is prepared to go to extremes to hire you. When this happens you will know you are WANTED.

38

AIM TO BE WORD AND FACT PERFECT

The only way to become perfect is to be imperfect in the first place

Aim for perfection in what you say. Only talk about what you know. Ensure what you know is reality. To achieve perfection (10/10 when tested) always do your homework.

A minority of bullshitters have made it to the top. But it is best to know what you are talking about if you want to enhance your career. Waffling and passing off opinions as fact will impress few.

Wise people are always able to provide evidence for their facts as well as elucidate each statement they make. They will avoid superlatives (which can rarely be substantiated) along with gross generalisations (which risk being meaningless).

Instead successful people do their homework with a view to being word and fact perfect. In doing so they develop a precious capability for distilling the essence from masses of data and voluminous reports. They also develop the ability to substantiate their argument, if challenged, by pinpointing the supporting facts.

Learning from mistakes leads to perfection

In striving to be word and fact perfect they refine the art of anticipating questions and devote time to compiling the key facts that will comprise the answers. When challenged, for example, on declining sales levels they will have the details available together with an assessment of the key factors that contribute to the decline. There will be no guesses, let alone the riding of hobby horses (for example, 'If only the HR department sorted out our compensation policies we wouldn't have this problem'). Instead they will state the facts: 'Our employee turnover has increased from 10–20 per cent in the last 12 months at the same time as we have reduced our training budgets. In my opinion these are contributory factors.'

People who pursue perfection in what they say rarely get caught out at interviews. They will have developed the skill of providing answers that are both credible and substantial.

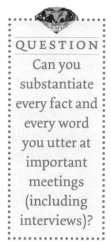

QUESTION
Can you substantiate every fact and every word you utter at important meetings (including interviews)?

Never allow yourself to become a 'bullshitter' who mouths platitudes, generalities and any old answer just for the sake of it. These people might sound plausible with their 'gift of the gab', but ultimately senior people will see through them and discover them for what they are, 'All surface and no substance'. When you are close to being word and fact perfect you will have substance and be much wanted.

PRACTICAL TIPS

To become perfect you must:

- identify and eliminate in the first instance your own imperfections (such as mouthing platitudes, passing off clichés as your own wisdom, presenting opinions and assumptions as facts or using ambiguities and amphibologies);
- accept gracefully the errors you make and use them as great learning opportunities;
- ensure you are able to substantiate everything you say or write.

To practise this rewrite the following using your own examples:

- 'When I stated that we have reduced costs by 5 per cent in our department I was referring to the year-on-year figures in our regular financial reports.'
- 'My recommendation of Bertie Reynolds as the best sales representative in the region was based on his track record in sales over the last three years and his excellent relationships with customers, old and new.'
- 'My calculation was based on the exchange rate in the *Financial Times* last Thursday when I wrote the report.'

39

MAKE
SACRIFICES

The pleasure always comes last. The pain comes first

Ask yourself, 'What am I prepared to sacrifice to protect my job and take my career further forward?' (NB Never sacrifice safety, hygiene or morality.) The pleasures you give up are your 'sacrifice'.

Little can be achieved in life without sacrificing something pleasurable. Marathon athletes make considerable sacrifices to achieve their ambition. Instead of lying in bed they take long runs. This is synonymous with long-term career progression. The pain is always front-end loaded with the benefit attained on completion. It can never be the other way round.

There is no gain without personal sacrifice

To become wanted by any organisation you have to do more than your competitors. This means sacrificing the television and many of the comforts indulged in at home. It might even mean less time with your family.

Inevitably this brings serious conflicts along the scale of the now fashionable 'work–life balance'. The harsh reality of life is that those who make sacrifices and work harder than the rest will triumph over those who relapse into comfort zones and put in fewer hours.

No matter how much you try you cannot progress your career on a 35-hour working week. The trick, as stated in Chapter 1, is to fall in love with your work such that it is fun and you are prepared to sacrifice other indulgences in favour of dedicating extra hours working hard at things you love doing. Gardening might be hard work, but those who love it are prepared to undertake the arduous tasks of weeding and pruning in order to achieve immense beauty.

When it comes to those critical moments in your career, when prospective employers have to make choices, their inclination will always be to select candidates who have made sacrifices to be where they are. It's called 'putting yourself out for the company' and is the reverse of the '9–5' mentality.

Whether you are an ambitious 18-year-old student or a 50-year-old just made redundant you will need to face the reality that sacrifices have to be made in pursuit of your long-term career goals. It might mean earning less to begin with, or putting in extra hours of study, or living away from your family for an extended period. Nothing is easy in life – and people who believe otherwise delude themselves. Be prepared to make sacrifices if you want to progress your career.

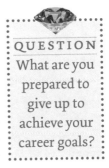

QUESTION

What are you prepared to give up to achieve your career goals?

PRACTICAL TIPS

- Watching a lot of television will do you little good. Sacrifice viewing and spend the time more productively in pursuit of your career goals.
- Be prepared to be lonely as you travel towards your career goals.
- Do not make a large salary your highest priority. There might be more noble objectives in becoming 'wanted'.
- Think twice before choosing the easiest and most comfortable option.

40

WORK FOR
DICTATORS

One year working for a dictator is worth two years at business school

Don't become a dictator but work for one, just for the wonderful experience.

Dictators make all the decisions. They micromanage. They only listen to a handful of people in their inner circle. They are insensitive to people's feelings and do not tolerate fools (who they define as not having to hand the answers they want). Most times dictators are volatile, unpredictable and irrational. They are prone to the worst excesses of emotional outrage.

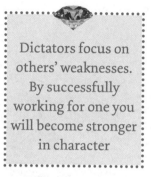

Dictators focus on others' weaknesses. By successfully working for one you will become stronger in character

As such they are excellent bosses to work for. In a perverse way you can learn much from them and also about yourself. You'll learn how to stand up to bullies.

I recall one dictator I worked for. His terrible reputation preceded him. Most people were terrorised by his extreme autocratic tendencies and I was warned about joining his team (if you could call them that). His induction technique was to drop you in the deep end and then seek out and expose the first mistake you made along with any weakness he perceived in you. He would punish you by rubbing your nose in the mire and humiliating you, often in front of others. He would frequently test his team by making unreasonable requests, for example by calling us up at 9 pm and instructing us to attend an urgent meeting in his office at 11 pm.

Indirectly he taught me to keep on my toes and be alert all the time. He would not tolerate waffle so I had to be fact and figure perfect as well as completely up to date every moment of the day (and night). I also learnt that the only way to disagree with him was to be 100 per cent sure of my case. He would then listen and sometimes agree. In this way I slowly gained his respect. After a while he took the pressure off me and ceased exposing my failings. I had entered his inner circle. Meanwhile he had started bullying another rookie.

What dictators do inadvertently is sort out the 'men from the boys' or the 'wheat from the chaff'. You get to know whether you are weak or strong in the face of exceptionally dominant bosses. Weaker team members fade away and foment dissent in the employee restaurant. Those who are strong grow apace and learn many things. They learn how to deal with irrational bosses (and there are more around than you think). They learn how to respond to personal insults (by becoming stronger – dictators only insult the weakest). They learn to be very good at their job by focusing on what is important at the same time as having an excellent grasp of the detail.

And of course by working for a dictator you learn the all-important technique of 'playing the game'. You learn to laugh at the dictator's jokes and only to make jokes the dictator will laugh at. You learn to say the right thing and avoid statements that will spark a choleric outburst of rage. You learn how to humour him as well as sense his every mood in the broad spectrum of unpredictable emotions he displays. In return you will be taken into the dictator's confidence and learn all the hot gossip first.

This is stuff they don't normally teach you in management and motivation classes but it is vital for your personal development if you want to become the person that every boss wants.

PRACTICAL TIPS

- When a dictator insults or abuses you never take it personally. Remember that he or she is the person with the problem, not you.
- Never reveal your weaknesses to a dictator.
- Remember that all dictators have been successful in getting themselves into a position of power. Thus with rare exceptions all dictators have their good points. Make a note of these and learn accordingly. Similarly make a note of their many bad points – and learn not to adopt these.
- Never work for a tyrant. There is a difference. (Check your dictionary!)

Career stimuli　9

QUIRKS

- The Q-factor: odd, eccentric, peculiar, curious, whimsical, variable, cranky, non-conformist, unusual, unorthodox, dissident, deviant, bizarre, atypical, bohemian, aberrational, unfashionable, strange, freakish, idiosyncratic, kinky, fanciful, rebellious, weird, surreal, avant-garde, unfamiliar, unconventional, iconoclastic, queer, heretical, heterodox, challenging, foibles, megrims, exceptions, square peg, oddball, contrary, off-beat, uncustomary, anomalous, non-aligned, surprising, non-standard, capricious, faddish, wayward, mercurial, irrational.
- Quirkiness colours an organisation.
- Without quirkiness an organisation is grey.
- Colour your job and career with some quirks.
- It is the people who are colourful who are WANTED.

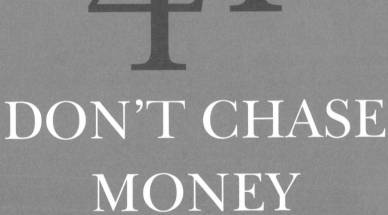

41

DON'T CHASE MONEY

Money is unpredictable. Far better to focus on the non-financials

Forget about money for a few days. You'll become incredibly motivated and happy. It is the 'power of now'.

During any recession the happiest people are those who do not worry about money. This does not mean they have a lot of money. It means they have more important things on their mind and are not driven by the fear and greed that comprise a mania for money.

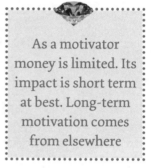

As a motivator money is limited. Its impact is short term at best. Long-term motivation comes from elsewhere

It might be a surprise but those bosses who focus on these more important things are more likely to make money than those who focus only on money. When you were 10 years old and pleading for more pocket money your parents will probably have told you, 'The best things in life are free', or, 'Money does not bring happiness'. Your parents were right!

Speaking at a conference in London on 10 October 2001 one of the most successful chief executives in the world, now retired, Jack Welch said: 'Profit is not an end in itself but a product of having a great team of people do a great job. In the end it's all about people. That was my job at General Electric.'

You will hear the same message from other successful chief executives. In fact I heard Bill Ford (Chairman of the Ford Motor Company) say it on televison this evening. Business is all about people, it is not about money. In this modern age profit results from having an organisation of highly motivated and talented people. The financiers who chase money might make a lot of it in the short term but in the long term they risk going the way of many Wall Street experts. Broke.

If you want to convince anyone of your suitability for a job then do not talk money. Too much focus on money is demeaning and degrading in a corporate world where the accent should be on environmental issues, customer satisfaction, community, inspirational management and happy employees. At home most people spend a couple of hours every week checking their bank statements and paying their bills. The rest of their time they do more important things such as play with the kids and have meals with the family. The same ratio should apply to work: no more than 5 per cent of your time should be spent on financial administration. The rest of your time should be dedicated to colleagues, customers and the community.

The obsession with money is a commercial psychosis you should not allow to distort your mind. Instead devote 95 per cent of your energies at work to non-financial matters. One successful chief executive told me: 'I find all that financial stuff so boring that I leave it the finance people to handle. They know perfectly well when to come to me for a decision. What we do is agree financial targets and a budget for the year, division by division, and then I let everyone get on with it. All I get is summary weekly and monthly financial reports. That's enough for me. I know when to take action. I am well advised by the experts.'

The sad fact of life is that any obsession with money is guaranteed to bring disappointment. Money is ephemeral and too often a major distraction on the road to happiness.

PRACTICAL TIPS

- Devote 95 per cent of your waking hours to non-financial matters.
- Give some money away every day and see how you feel. (See also Chapter 13.)
- If you don't feel good then give even more away the next day. Keep on giving more and more until you really do feel good. (*A fair percentage of the money you have you don't need!*)

42

EXPERIMENT
WITH
IRRATIONALITY

Irrational thinking is at the root of much success

Experiment with irrationality in addressing seemingly intractable problems. Work is an art form and requires a trip beyond the bounds of reason to make progress.

Together the USA's White House and Wall Street have the financial clout to hire the best brains in the world. But even these, with all their powers of rational thinking, could not prevent the 2008/2009 recession. The solution of 'stimulus packages' would have seemed irrational two years earlier.

In creating future direction rationality is as limited as a set of railway lines. In his book *Against the Odds*[1] Sir James Dyson writes: 'There are 5 billion people out there thinking in train tracks, and thinking what they have been taught to think. Be illogical. Half the time people will laugh at you and half the time you will strike up something interesting.' When he first attempted to invent the dual cyclone bagless vacuum cleaner he received little support (especially from the major banks) for his apparently irrational business proposition. The same applied to Herb Kelleher, who pioneered Southwest Airlines, one of the first low-cost airlines. Everyone thought he was *Nuts*[2] (the title of a book about him). He's been a great success.

What is reasonable to you can be unreasonable to others (and vice versa)

---

[1] *Against the Odds*, James Dyson, Orion Publishers, 1997

[2] *Nuts - The Story of Herb Kelleher and Southwest Airlines*, Kevin Freiberg & Jackie Freiberg, Bard Press, 1996

The constraints of rationality extend way back in history. For example just under 500 years ago Queen Elizabeth I was reputed to have said: 'I take a bath once a month, even if I do not need to.' This is how she (the top person in England) reasoned about personal hygiene. In 1874 Alexander Graham Bell demonstrated his invention of the telephone to Queen Victoria. 'I can't imagine why anyone would want to use this contraption', she remarked. This was her rationality: she saw no need for the development and use of the telephone.

In his book *Predictably Irrational*[3] Dan Ariely gives many examples of people's irrational behaviour, for example in making purchasing decisions. Other experts would also assert that human beings are much more irrational than rational. Furthermore they would assert that irrationality drives the creative process and leads to progress.

Rationality along with reason is a peculiar concept. We attribute it to ourselves but criticise others for lack of it. We tend to believe that whatever we do is rational or reasonable whilst what others do (especially politicians and often senior executives) is irrational or unreasonable. This in itself is irrational. What is rational to us is often irrational to others.

There is no such thing as absolute reason or rationality. If there were it would be called 'logic'. Logic is a process underpinned by scientific validation leading to a conclusion that can be proved. It is based on clear evidence.

Creativity is totally divorced from logic, reason and rationality. Therefore to make progress in any field of endeavour it is necessary to experiment with irrationality. A classic case is the invention by 3M of Post-it notes. These were not the result of

---

rational thinking but rather the irrational consequence of a scientific experiment that went wrong.

It is thus rational to be irrational and to experiment with different thought processes. In a democracy such freedom to think differently (and express oneself accordingly) is treasured.

There is much historical evidence that being irrational (or even unreasonable) leads to immense creativity. As I write I am listening to Tchaikovsky's Piano Concerto No.1. When in 1874 Peter Tchaikovsky asked his mentor Nikolai Rubinstein for an opinion of the draft composition the celebrated Moscow pianist commented, 'Your concerto is worthless, unplayable, hackneyed, clumsy, beyond correction, trivial and vulgar.' Rubinstein considered it unreasonable to expect any concert pianist to play it. Tchaikovsky walked out on his friend and resolved not to change a note in the score. He persuaded another pianist, Hans von Bülow, to give the first performance. Rubinstein later admitted his rational judgement had been in error and subsequently became a fan of the work. Today the concerto is the most popular in the repertoire.

Experimenting with irrationality leads to great debate and even better decisions. It simply requires that you start thinking in a way that counters current rationality. It means that you have to challenge your perceptions, interpretations, emotions and beliefs – especially those you hold which are conventional. It also means that you challenge those of others too.

The best organisations therefore encourage dissent providing it is not aimed at hurting colleagues. It is the 'reason' that should be challenged, not the person. As mentioned previously President Abraham Lincoln and subsequently President Barack Obama described this as 'creating a team of rivals'.

'Convention' is the embodiment of rationalities that the majority accept whilst the 'unconventional' go beyond the bounds of normal reasoning. Examples are manifold. Thus Apple Computers was not invented by a meticulously rational IBM, the largest computer manufacturer at the time. Google was not invented by Microsoft, the phenomenally successful developer of Windows software. Amazon.com was not invented by a large chain of bookstores such as Borders or Barnes & Noble. The larger companies become the more they attempt to exercise strategic rationality, but this can be at the price of creativity and the innovations of seemingly unreasonable people.

If you are totally rational you risk being totally predictable and this will not be wanted. Progress arises when people behave unpredictably and irrationally.

PRACTICAL TIPS

- Challenge yourself: 'Is there a different set of rationalities I can apply here?'
- Experiment with the idea of being irrational in finding solutions.
- Challenge reasons for problems and find an alternative set of reasons for finding a solution.

43
DO MENTAL CALLISTHENICS

Strengthen your career by strengthening your mind

Challenge your brain cells daily. Undertake at least one mental exercise every morning, for example try multiplying 59×59^1 in your head.

A few decades ago one of my teachers emphasised that the brain was a muscle which needed exercising and strengthening on a regular basis – otherwise it would atrophy and get flabby. He encouraged mental arithmetic and would suggest: 'When you leave school learn for example the 14 times table or multiply 23×23 in your head.' He asserted that by doing so our brain power would be increased. He also proposed reading classic literature and other books many found unreadable. He mentioned for example James Joyce's *Ulysses* and said it would be helpful to know who Leopold Bloom and Stephen Dedalus were, if we were ever asked.

Expressed another way, a lazy brain leads to a lazy life whilst an active brain will lead to an active career. Activating your brain with increasingly difficult challenges will certainly strengthen your mind and prepare you for those awkward questions interviewers throw at career-climbers, such as: 'What is your favourite character in classical literature?' or 'In your existing job if you were given an extra million in your budget what would you do with it?'

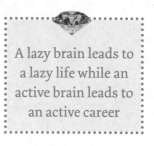

A lazy brain leads to a lazy life while an active brain leads to an active career

Some people rely on crosswords or Sudoku to sharpen up, although these can be too narrowly focused for broad-band intel-

---

[1] To obtain the answer easily multiply 60×60, subtract 60 and then subtract 59

ligence. Knowing the download speeds for the Internet in various countries can help – especially when your boss is frustrated with the exorbitantly expensive and frustratingly slow 256 kbytes he experienced on his recent trip to an 'emerging country'.

Watching the soaps and reading the tabloids is definitely worthwhile if you want to understand the masses, but possibly not worth mentioning at an interview. A knowledge of sport will definitely help, especially if you can establish that your interviewer's favourite team is the one you support too. (A little detective work here is evidence of an enquiring mind and will definitely help.)

At one London University a concierge learnt to say 'Good Morning' and 'Good Night' in 20 different languages so that he could say a few words in their local language to the large number of foreign students attending the university. At a resort in Mauritius a porter, a football fanatic, would check the Internet every Saturday night and memorise all the football scores in the UK Premier League (along with the major European leagues) so that he could inform visitors arriving Sunday morning after a long overnight flight of the score of the team they supported. He would even memorise who scored the goals. 'Which football team do you support?' he would ask. 'Manchester United.' 'They won 1–0 yesterday. Rooney scored.' What a start to a holiday!

In summary, the number of ways to strengthen your mind is infinite. Sadly many people do not get beyond 'point zero' and come to nothing as a result.

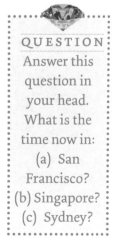

QUESTION
Answer this
question in
your head.
What is the
time now in:
(a) San
Francisco?
(b) Singapore?
(c) Sydney?

PRACTICAL TIPS

- Study the financial pages of the more serious newspapers and familiarise yourself with economic trends, for example of the main countries in Asia.
- Check exchange rates daily so that you know how to convert dollars into Chinese renminbi as well as pounds into euros.
- Learn some basic Chinese words in order to offer greetings to your Chinese suppliers.
- Memorise the names of everyone you meet when visiting a new company.

Career stimuli **10**

REINFORCEMENTS

- Back up your learning in the way you back up the files on your laptop.
- Few things are learnt the first time.
- Lessons have to be reinforced.
- Reinforce yourself by review, reflection and reinstatement.
- Reinforce yourself by recharging your 'self'.
- Reinforce your 'self' by renewing yourself.
- To take two steps forward take one step back.
- The force in your career comes from reinforcement.
- Maximise the reinforcement in your job and in your career to be WANTED.

44

TRAVEL THE WORLD

Go to Ouagadougou (the capital of a country called ... ... that was previously called ... ...). Expand your mind

Set yourself a personal goal of making at least two overseas working trips each year. If your organisation doesn't cooperate then don't limit yourself there. Find a progressive employer who is open minded and encourages travel in order to develop the business and the ambitious people within it.

One of my early career ambitions was to travel the world at my employer's expense. I achieved this. If that is your ambition too then this is the chapter to wave in front of your boss (assuming he or she is not on assignment in Ouagadougou).

People who never move outside their village during their lives develop what I call 'village mentality'. They have limited horizons and see things only in terms of what is happening in their village. The same applies to employees or managers who spend all their career working in the same place for the same company. 'Village mentality' is then named 'institutionalisation'.

People with 'village mentality' have limited horizons

Conversely those who travel the world have the opportunity to gain global perspectives and real understanding of different cultures. This positions them well in their careers when it comes to reaching out for broad-spanning jobs that embrace the complexities demanded of a triple-seven mind. International travel colours a person, adding a third dimension of deep and vivid experience to a knowledge that comprises no more than an outline sketch in the minds of those who have never travelled.

Travel also brings oodles of motivation and a kudos amongst colleagues, friends and family. 'I'm sorry my daughter can't be with us this evening, but yesterday she popped across to San Francisco for an important business meeting. She should be back tomorrow.'

Travelling the world brings experiences you've never dreamt of and that you can put to good use in entertaining those old bores back in the office. It is a cliché to state that we now live in a global world. Any professional person should therefore be able to include achievements in various parts of the globe on his or her CV.

So if you haven't done so already now is the time to 'get on your bike' (as Baron Norman Tebbit famously once said), take a ride to the airport and fly off to confront the biggest overseas challenge your department has. Alternatively just book yourself a place at an important conference on the other side of the world. Ignore those miserable sods back home who call it a 'jolly' or a 'jaunt'. Even though you will definitely have fun you will still learn an immense amount, hopefully achieve much and after a few days return home a better person. What more could anyone want? How could I be sitting here in the Philippines writing this if I had not practised what I preach? I've just returned from presenting in four different cities in China, and before that I was in Mauritius. Next month I'll be making one of my regular visits to Singapore and then it's another trip to China. Later this year will find me in South Africa for the 'nth' time. Travel opens up vistas in the mind you could not previously imagine. It gives you confidence too.

Travel opens up vistas in your mind you could not previously imagine

PRACTICAL TIPS

- Keep a travel journal.
- Take notes.
- Jot down key lessons and look for the best in every country you visit – even if it is the worst in the world (and there is one).
- Learn to say 'Hello, how are you?' and 'Thank you' in the language of the country you are visiting.
- Memorise some basic facts about the country you will be visiting (recent history, the name of the president, etc.).

45

BE LOYAL TO
YOURSELF

There is very little value in company loyalty

Only be loyal to yourself, family and friends – not to your company. When the financial crunch comes your employer will rarely be loyal to you.

Here is an email I opened earlier today: '*Dear David, Just to inform you that my time at Company XXX is coming to an end as my position has been axed as a result of the credit crunch...*' I have had quite a few similar emails over recent weeks.

I am old enough to have worked through a number of recessions. On one occasion my company's CEO returned from our multinational's head office to report that the group president had decided upon a 20 per

When the crunch comes it's the loyal who get fired

cent job cut across the board due to a dire financial situation. It was the proverbial blunt axe. There were to be no exceptions.

I was vice-president, Human Resources (HR) reporting to the CEO and I quickly started implementing a previously agreed voluntary severance programme for front-liners, supervisors and middle managers. This worked to good effect. The problem was with the ten executives of the top team – of which I was one. The CEO insisted that in all fairness two of us had to go. Only one of my colleagues volunteered to 'take the money' and leave. So the CEO insisted on the compulsory termination of one of the remaining nine. Fortunately it was not me. Having previously alerted me (as head of HR) the CEO called the victim into his office and fired the bullet. He then quickly directed the shattered man to my office to pick up the pieces and do the necessary touchy-feely stuff that HR people are apparently expert in.

The victim was in a terrible state of shock. He was crying and trembling. He was suffering an emotional breakdown. 'I joined this company when I was 16,' he told me in between sobs. 'For 38 years I have given this company my life, working excessive hours and doing my best for each and every chief executive. Nobody has ever complained about my work and what I have achieved. I worked so hard for this company my first marriage broke up. I remarried four years ago and have 3-year-old twins to support. Now this... I just don't understand.'

I understood. When it comes to the crunch there is no mercy in business. There is no premium on loyalty. 'Company loyalty' is a misnomer. You cannot be loyal to a legal concept (a company). You can only be loyal to people, and normally these are people who are loyal to you – such as members of your family. When the financial losses are counted companies just cannot be loyal to their employees.

Professing years of company loyalty adds very little value in any race for promotion or any application for a good job. Stressing to a potentially new employer your 'loyalty' when you are trying to leave your old company will seem strange. Similarly your existing company is not going to try to hold on to you if it knows you are never going to leave. In that sense you pose no threat to the future of the enterprise. Loyalty to a company is rarely valued.

Conversely those ambitious people who have the potential to move to a competitor (and thus demonstrate disloyalty) are more likely to be wooed by their current employer than the poor loyal people who never present any threat.

The ultimate loyalty must be to your family and it is essential you assign the highest priority to them. This means that there are occasions when you have to be disloyal to your current employer, and leave for a better job.

PRACTICAL TIPS

- Do not allow yourself to be branded at work as a loyal company man (or woman). You will be taken advantage of and not valued.
- Remember that we live in a harsh competitive world where people lose out through no fault of their own.
- Remember that if you want to win in such an aggressive world you must put yourself first.
- Remember that when you become wanted it is not just a matter of you competing for a job but of an employer competing for you.

46

DO SOMETHING NEW EVERY DAY

Enhance your mental fitness by doing new things

Frequently find new ways. Whatever you and your colleagues do continually ask the question: 'Is there a new and better way of doing this?'

> The more new things you do the more new experiences you will have and the wiser you will become

An antidote to ageing is renewal. It has a limited effect on the body but can work wonders on your mind. Such renewal will be reflected through the shine in your eyes. People with dull eyes never renew themselves. They never think new thoughts and never attempt to do new things.

The people who are wanted in most organisations are those who can think anew and do new things to improve the performance of the business. They are always exploring new options for replacing the less efficient and discredited modus operandi. It is a fact of life that whatever you do, and whatever is done by your company, there is always a better way to do it. If you don't find that better way then someone else will and you risk losing your job and your company going out of business.

Doing new things brings vitality, freshness, motivation and the possibility of improvement whilst repetition of old things brings routine, dullness and the impossibility of innovation.

The challenge in doing new things is to start thinking in new ways. Repetitive thinking is dangerous as it can lead to a non-thinking, subconscious approach to your work. Instead you should perhaps think of new ways of communicating with your colleagues rather than by the usual email or text messaging.

Think too of new ways of spending time with your colleagues as well as your customers and suppliers.

Here are some examples of new things other people do:

- Veronica Ferguson on reception is always looking for new ways of welcoming visitors.
- Ingrid Christensen challenges her team to produce one exciting new idea every month.
- Using the Internet Mohammad Khan reads a new newspaper every day with a view to learning one new thing.
- With over 200 branches in his company Ivan Fischer visits one new branch every week.
- Twice a week Jane Zanowski will take her lunch tray and sit at a table with people she doesn't know. She will ask a few questions, listen and learn anew.
- Sally Kershaw arrives at work at a new time every morning.
- Bill Kirby strives to chat to one new person (he doesn't know) every day.
- Adrian Smith finds new ways every month of running his team meeting.
- Maria Perez is always seeking new ways of obtaining feedback from her customers.
- Martha Tan takes a new route through the large open-plan office every morning, stopping to chat briefly with one new person every time.
- Arnold Nkosi looks for new non-financial rewards for best performers every quarter.

By keeping 'new' you increase the probability of some great new idea emerging that can revolutionise your company, whether it be a new product, a new design or a new way of distributing your goods to customers. You can also think of new ways of furthering your career. Everything is possible, albeit not everything new is obvious. By keeping fresh and thinking anew you will begin to see things in different ways. This will give you ideas for innovation and improvement. These creative new ideas can never be a result of rational thought. Instead they tend to 'bubble through' to your consciousness when your mind is alive to new possibilities. This means talking with new people, doing new things and exposing yourself to new experiences. It was in this way that Starbucks (as we know it today) was founded by Howard Schultz. The same can be said of Amazon and Jeff Bezos, Virgin and Sir Richard Branson. The rational thinking came later. The new idea bubbled up first.

PRACTICAL TIPS

- Meet informally with your colleagues and have only one item on the agenda: 'What can we do anew?'
- Follow your instinct, express your feelings and keep sparking.
- Challenge yourself to do one new thing every day.
- Examine new things that have revolutionised the world (e.g. Google, the iPod) and find out where these new ideas came from.

47

WORK HARD

If it's easy it's not work

Start early, finish late, make the extra effort and don't waste time doing nothing when at work. Work is good for you and hard work even better. Without work you'll be begging the state for financial assistance. Do everything possible to avoid this. Work so hard it hurts! Then stop.

In December 2008 Britain's oldest worker died at the age of 105. Jim Webber was a gardener and only stopped work at 104 when autumn came and the coldness and damp afflicted his arthritis. 'It was his love of

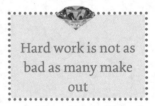

Hard work is not as bad as many make out

working outside that kept him going so long', his daughter Kathy told the *Western Morning News*. He lived in Stoke Abbot, Dorset, and worked for village residents and the local pub, the New Inn, mowing lawns, trimming hedges and doing general gardening.

One could conclude from the above story that hard work hurt no one. Even so life is hard and work is hard. In fact for millions of people getting work is hard enough, let alone feeding their families and putting a roof over their heads. This becomes particularly acute during a recession.

The opportunity to work should be prized and not discarded by a lazy 'can't be bothered' attitude. We all recognise hard work when we see it. Two years ago I emigrated from the UK. The two men who came to help me pack up all my possessions and have them shipped abroad worked incredibly hard. I saw no slacking off. Instead I saw the sweat on their brows. But come the end of a late working day they were smiling and proud they had accomplished a good job done. What they did in one day others would take two days over and charge twice as much for. In the end it is those who work hard that prosper.

There is a prevailing ethos in Western society that work is 'bad' and to be avoided. That is why there are pressures for shorter working weeks and longer vacations and why many complain of that 'Monday morning feeling' and 'I can't wait till Friday'. Weekends and public holidays are seen as good whilst working days are seen as 'bad'. This resistance to work is catching and creates an attitude whereby employees do the bare minimum as specified in their employment contract. One can argue the case for basic hours and 'work to rule', but the reality of global competition is that those who work hardest prosper most.

Hard work does not mean allowing yourself to be exploited. It does mean making every effort to achieve the results your company expects, and more if you wish. People will know when they are being exploited by excessive demands for excessive hours or for 'doing the jobs of two people'. Hard work is voluntary and is not only for the good of the organisation but for your own good. Hard work helps progress your career as you can demonstrate a greater contribution than others when competing for promotion.

Hard work is an attitude of mind and reflects the determined effort you are prepared to make to stay in a job as well as to become that 'hard-working person everyone wants'. To quote the TV presenter Sir Michael Parkinson in an interview in the *Daily Telegraph* (4 December 2008): 'The route to the top is not to go on *X-Factor* but, as Madonna pointed out, "to work bloody hard at your job – as all great artists do".'

Inevitably there is a line to be drawn. Workaholics risk burnout and are vulnerable to all sorts of maladies and social ills. Tired people also make bad (if not dangerous) decisions. Only you can draw that line. Your body, mind and heart (if not your spouse and family) will tell you when to 'stop' – when enough is enough. Even so our capacity for hard work is high, and for many the boundaries can always be pushed further. As mentioned previously if you love your work then you will hardly see it as work. It will become your vocation and your mission, to which you devote most of your waking hours during weekdays (and sometimes Saturdays too). But as the wise man said right at the beginning, 'Do take one day off every week'.

PRACTICAL TIPS

- Do not allow yourself to be subjected to negative peer pressure such that your work rate is reduced to the lowest common denominator.
- It is no sin to work harder than your colleagues.

48

BE CURIOUS

When you ask questions you get answers. When you ask no questions you get no answers – and you never learn

Question everything and everyone, including yourself.

At a conference in London on 23 May 2002 a member of the audience asked the speaker, 'Michael, you are 37 years old. You are one of the richest men in the world. I just want to know what

> Curiosity is a prime motivational driver

motivates you? What gets you out of bed in the morning? Why do you keep on working when you have all the money in the world?'

The speaker Michael Dell's answer was fascinating. 'What motivates me is curiosity,' he replied. 'I believe there is always a better way to do things. So I am always curious – how can I find a better way? I bought my first computer, an Apple Mac, when I was 15 years old. I was curious how it worked. So I took it apart. Then I found a better way to make computers. Then I found a better way to sell computers.'

On BBC Radio 3 on 24 March 2005 there was a feature on Sir Harry Kroto (winner of the 1996 Nobel Prize for Chemistry). He gave a quotation from the year 1123. It was from Adelard of Bath, the twelfth-century English scholar: 'Give me the freedom to doubt and I will question. By questioning I will arrive at the truth.' Such is curiosity.

A dominant characteristic of many ambitious people is their curiosity. They are always asking themselves questions such as, 'How can I improve?' or 'How do I get the job I want?' or 'How can I keep up to date?'

Thus if you are a teacher aspiring to be a head teacher you should question yourself: 'How do I get a headship?' and 'Why not the top job for me in due course? There are obviously many who get to where I want to be.' By becoming curious any person can work out the course needed to get there – 'there' being the appointment that fulfils their ambition.

Curiosity then becomes a habit. It becomes a daily process of asking questions, of exploration, of research to determine the route necessary.

The world's number one golfer during the last decade, Tiger Woods, does not rest on his laurels. Having won his first US Masters in 1997 by a record margin of 12 strokes the first question he asked himself was: 'How can I improve my swing?' Successful people are always questioning themselves: 'How can I do better?'

From my teenage days one of my ambitions was to have a book published. This ambition kept recurring in my mind as a picture: my first book on display in the window of Foyles Bookstore, Charing Cross Road, London. I soon realised there was no

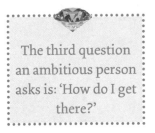

The third question an ambitious person asks is: 'How do I get there?'

straightforward and easy route to accomplishing this. So I asked myself the question, 'How do I get there?' My curiosity led to the answer. Whilst I experienced many 'dead-ends' (rejections) I eventually achieved what I wanted, the publication of my first book, *Superboss* [1], and it being featured in the Foyles' window. I found a way because I was curious enough to find a way.

In summary, to become 'wanted' you must be curious and keep asking yourself, 'What do I want of myself?', 'What will others want of me when I get there?' and finally, 'How do I get there?'

---

[1] *Superboss*, David Freemantle, Gower, 1985

PRACTICAL TIPS

- Be curious and question everything that puzzles you.
- Never be afraid to ask questions.
- When you meet successful people be curious and be forward.
- Ask them how they got there. At best you will get answers, at worst none.
- Never be personal when asking questions. Always start by asking innocuous questions to satisfy your curiosity. Then, once you get to know someone, you can venture forward with more risky questions.
- Never pose negative questions (which imply deficiencies or mistakes).
- The best questions are those that seek lessons from the person you are questioning.

49

ACQUIRE A
SECOND STRING

Never rely on the skills and knowledge you have. Develop new skills. Acquire new knowledge

The more options you can offer (in terms of skills, knowledge and experience) the higher the probability you will be wanted.

Alexander McCall Smith (already mentioned in Chapter 21) is not only a best-selling author and great speaker but also an amateur bassoonist. But his main job has been as a professor of Medical Law. Benjamin Zander (see Chapter 21 again) started his life in music but now also lectures as a leadership and motivational guru. They have both acquired second strings to their bow.

We all understand the need for insurance but often neglect this when it comes to the worst thing that can happen to us at work – losing our jobs. Every day there are news reports of companies scaling back on their operations and making thousands of staff redundant. I feel sorry for these people, especially those who have failed to prepare for this eventuality and don't have the insurance of alternative career paths.

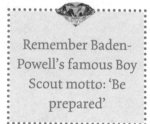

Remember Baden-Powell's famous Boy Scout motto: 'Be prepared'

When a company's revenues and profits drop substantially it has no option but to fire employees. It is a harsh but regrettable fact of life.

Any employee's first priority must be to safeguard his future, protect the welfare of his family and ensure he is well positioned to seize the first opportunity to regain employment. Apart from any 'job-loss' insurance scheme this priority requires two further types of insurance. The first is to view the redundancy positively. Your initial reaction might be, as stated earlier, 'This is the worst thing that has happened to me – I've lost my job' but within 24 hours you should have transformed your thinking such that: 'This is the best thing that has happened to me – it gives me a golden opportunity for a fresh start in my career.' Positive thinking about setbacks is great insurance against a desperate future.

The second form of insurance is to acquire a second string to your bow. Wise people are never complacent, nor do they rely on a narrow experience and skills base for generating income. To be prepared for the future it is essential to work hard at developing a second set of skills so that if you are made redundant you will have more options. This might mean, for example, gaining experience in teaching or training in addition to your original profession. It might mean learning a new language so that you have more appeal to any employer operating globally. It might mean doing something completely different, for example studying alternative medicine in your spare time in order to be well positioned to make a career of this in the future, should you so wish.

Furthermore, by acquiring a second string to your bow you will have more to offer a prospective employer who might want someone who can devote one day a week to in-house training in addition to practising their specialism.

Pete Jimenez's week-day job is as general manager of Optima Digital in the Philippines. However he has acquired a second string to his bow. During weekends he roams the junk shops of Mandaluyong and Quezon City searching for scrap iron, rusty pipes, nails and any metal parts that set his imagination working. He then converts these into metal sculptures. 'I work in my garage. I never know what sculptures I'm going to make because I never know what scrap iron I'm going to find', he says. His sculptures have been widely exhibited. 'If his company ever puts Pete on the scrap heap,' commented a fan, 'he'll know exactly what to do.'

People who limit themselves to one professional skill set risk being categorised as too narrow in outlook. More often nowadays employers are looking for people who are multiskilled and thus sufficiently versatile to adapt to changing business requirements.

PRACTICAL TIPS

- Review the skills, knowledge and experience you require for your current job and ask yourself: 'Would I have to rely on these to get another job?'
- If the answer is 'yes' think seriously about acquiring a second string to your bow.
- This can relate to anything that really fascinates you.
- Then devote time and energy to acquiring this new set of skills.

50

CREATE
POSSIBILITIES

If you tell yourself 'It's impossible' then it will be. Whatever you want from work and in your career is possible only if you tell yourself it is. This also requires optimism and hope

Explore the possibilities of progress, of improvements, of a better future for you, your family and the organisation you want to work for.

On 15 August 1620 the vessel the *Mayflower* left the port of Southampton, UK heading for the 'New World' of America. This involved a hazardous 66-day voyage across a stormy Atlantic. On arrival there were conflicts with indigenous Americans as well as the challenge of a bitterly cold winter and a hostile terrain. There was no guarantee that any of these brave people would survive, only the hope and possibility of a new future.

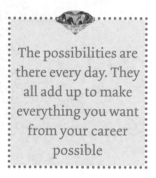

The possibilities are there every day. They all add up to make everything you want from your career possible

The same applies to any person migrating from one country to another or taking a new job in a town 100 miles from home. There can never be a guarantee of success, only possibilities and hope. Creating and pursuing a possibility can lead to failure, but equally it can lead to success. That's what the optimists believe.

Nelson Mandela spent 27 years in prison, much of that time in the notorious Robben Island jail off the coast of Cape Town, South Africa. He was an inspiration to his fellow prisoners. One thing he told them was: 'Do not see this as "The Prison of Robben Island" but as "The University of Robben Island".' Whilst the prison authorities practised hideous forms of psychological torture they did acquiesce to formal study. So some of the prisoners took distance learning courses whilst others just learnt to read and write. They would study long into the night, reading a textbook at night-time whilst sitting on the toilet – for that was where the only light bulb was shining. Some of his fellow prisoners went on to become judges or ministers in the new South African government after Nelson Mandela was released. Other prisoners became tour guides, and it was one of these who told me the above story during my visit to Robben Island. Nelson Mandela and his fellow prisoners suffered adversity and deprivation of an intensity and duration I hope neither you nor I ever experience. Despite the dreadful 27 years of incarceration Nelson Mandela helped people create possibilities by encouraging them to change their mindsets from negative to positive. When others had given up he saw the possibility of an end to apartheid. He saw the possibilities for every prisoner in terms of improvement and a brighter future. He saw optimism and hope everywhere.

Another example is Barack Obama, who saw the possibility of an African-American becoming president of the USA. When he initially touted the idea to some of his friends one or two said, 'America is not ready for you.' He proved them wrong.

A study of history will provide many other examples of determined people who pursued possibilities to make great progress in this world, despite the odds. The route to what you want, and what is wanted of you, can be long and arduous. What these people demonstrate is that even with the biggest obstacles and the severest setbacks everything is possible.

History also reveals that after things get worse they always get better. There is no stasis. To create possibilities of better things requires a huge dollop of optimism together with an abundance of hope. It is the optimists who succeed in life. They seek the light when all seems dark, see it, and are energised to create possibilities.

In the midst of the 2008 global financial crash Eric Schmidt, CEO of Google, was asked how his company was facing the recession. 'We're optimists,' replied Schmidt, 'we believe in the future. We believe in American creativity. We believe in possibilities. We believe in all the great things that got us as far as we have now. Those haven't gone away. We should be proud of what America has done. So let's get on with it. Let's get through this disaster and get back to business.'

Optimism brings hope, and with it the increased possibilities of turning your dream of a better future into reality. This is the underlying principle of Rhonda Byrne's best-selling book *The Secret*.[1] She calls it the 'law of attraction'. The eminent Austrian psychiatrist and Holocaust survivor, the late Viktor Frankl, revealed that those who gave up and became defeated had a higher possibility of dying in the concentration camps than the optimists who had hope.

Staying in a job and enjoying a successful career is all about optimism, hope and creating and pursuing possibilities that minimise the prospect of job loss and maximise the prospect of being wanted in any organisation. When external forces knock you down (for example losing your job during a recession) it is no good crying out, 'My situation is impossible.' The separatists who sailed on the *Mayflower* could easily have said, 'We are suffering repression in

Never throw a challenge to a pessimist. They never create possibilities

---

[1] *The Secret*, Rhonda Byrne, Atria Books, 2006

our homeland – our situation is impossible.' Instead they created possibilities by travelling to a new world.

The central theme of this book is that when it comes to your job and your career everything is possible[1], nothing is impossible. There will not be a single reader who is so devoid of skills, knowledge and experience that no employer will ever want him or her, whatever the economic situation in the world. Even if you are currently in prison or whether you have specific physical or mental limitations there is every possibility that out there, in the big wide world, is an employer who wants you, who will value the positive contribution you potentially offer.

---

[1] There is evidence enough of the assertion that 'everything is possible in your career'. As I undertook the final proof-reading of this book, the week beginning 12 April 2009, a wonderful example of 'possibility' hit the headlines around the world.

It relates to Susan Boyle from West Lothian in Scotland. She literally became an overnight sensation with her rendition of the song 'I Dreamed a Dream' on the TV show *Britain's Got Talent*. The video clip on YouTube has attracted tens of millions of hits and she has been interviewed on American TV.

Simply put, if Susan Boyle, 47, unemployed and rather frumpy looking can do it, so can you. You can achieve your career ambitions, you can become WANTED.